Daddy's Girl
Pat Kelley

© 2016 by Pat Kelley

Daddy's Girl

A memoir

First Edition, July 2016

Daddy's Girl is under copyright protection. No part of this book may be used or reproduced in any manner whatsoever without written permission except in the case of brief quotations embodied in critical articles and reviews. Printed in the United States of America. All rights reserved.

ISBN:

978-0-9968323-2-8

Cover photo is the author's fourth grade school picture. Photographer unknown

In Memoria

Willie Marie Purser Kelley was my mother, the first person who loved me without condition, and who showed me her love in every way she could. She was the world's best third-grade teacher, and loved her school children almost as much as she loved her birth children. When my brothers and I were in school plays, concerts or games, Mother was always there to support us and to remind us how much she loved us. As I recall, she never missed a one of my performances from the time I entered school until I graduated, and after I started teaching, she even came to the productions I directed.

Even when I was hurt, angry or frustrated with her, I always knew how much she loved me. Thank you, Mama.

Daddy's Girl

Chapter 1

I was twelve years old the day Daddy came in from working in the field and, following his usual routine, emptied the pockets of his khakis onto the piano bench in the living room. My two brothers and I were watching the *Mickey Mouse Club* on the black-and-white television. Mother was singing a hymn as she cooked supper in the adjacent kitchen. Daddy finished emptying his pockets, went to the bathroom, and took his bath.

When he finished, he put on clean clothes, returned to the piano bench, and began picking up the money he had left there. Suddenly, he stopped.

"Where's my money?"

Three pairs of frightened eyes stared up at him, but no one said a thing. Mother's melody died. We all sucked in a breath, waiting.

"I said, where's my money?" His voice was already rising, demanding, accusing. "It was there when I went to take my bath—now it's gone. Who took it?"

Silence.

"Who. Took. My. Money?"

The uncomfortable silence stretched. The atmosphere in the room was electric. Finally he charged over to me, grabbed my arm, and pulled me up into the middle of the room.

Facing my brothers, he said, "I know one of you boys took my money, and I don't think you'll let poor little Patricia take a whippin' for what you did, so this is your last chance." He tightened his grip. "Now, who took my money?"

We babbled all at once.

"I didn't do it, Daddy!" I cried.

"She didn't do nothin'!"

"Nobody did anything. We were all watchin' TV. Nobody even moved!"

Our pleas fell on deaf ears. Tears and snot ran down all three pale faces.

Mother stood in the doorway between the two rooms, a damp dishtowel crumpled in her hands, her own face wet with tears. "Short, you know they didn't take your money, now let her go." Her already timid voice was no more than a whisper.

"Shut up, Willie," he roared. "This ain't none o' your business!" He pulled off his thick leather belt, the one we had all felt at one time or another.

I whimpered. "No, Daddy, please!" The more I tried to pull away from him, the tighter he held me.

"Okay, I guess that's it, Tricia. You'll just have to take a whippin' for your brothers." He turned my limp body to face the large decorative mirror that hung on the wall over the couch, and watched himself beat me.

I screamed with the first lick. The panties and light cotton sundress I wore gave me little protection from each brutal blow. I howled and cried as he hit me again, and again, his excited eyes never leaving the mirror on the wall. It was a look I had seen many times before.

After more than a dozen excruciating licks, he pushed me back toward my seat and stomped into the bathroom. Mother helped me into my bedroom, stripped my bloody clothes, and cleaned my wounds. Blisters and bleeding cuts covered my buttocks and thighs. We cried together as she dressed those painful wounds and helped me get dressed again.

And then we all sat down to supper as if nothing had happened.

Chapter 2

Forty-five years later ...

I stood in front of an audience of professional women whose faces should have reflected their fascination with my presentation, "Success Secrets of the Masters." Instead, I saw only bowed heads and averted eyes, whispered questions, and pity. From the seminar sponsor's table, I heard committee members asking each other if they should just cancel the entire debacle as soon as possible.

In my mind, I saw the months of preparation as I researched, wrote, and rewrote my presentation, looking for just the right balance of practical skills and motivational stories. I wanted participants to leave the program excited about using new tools, or old tools newly discovered, to improve their lives. I spent countless hours memorizing and polishing my presentation, building in humor and pathos, drama and inspiration. I worked harder on this assignment than any I'd had in more than thirty years of delivering management training.

But it just wouldn't come together.

All those years of memorizing lines for my speeches and plays had made memorization easy for me, but now I couldn't remember the words to my own presentation. I used every spare moment studying the script, practicing gestures, trying to find some way to imprint the words into my brain. Nothing worked.

Two weeks before the scheduled date, I began having horrible, grotesque nightmares and losing sleep, and gained ten unwanted pounds. None of my clothes fit. I grew short-tempered; people began avoiding me. Finally, two days before the seminar, congestion tightened around my forehead and no amount of medication would soothe my dripping nose. It was a sinus infection.

The day of the seminar, I was in a medication-induced haze, exhausted, and completely unable to remember a single thing I had planned to say, but I snapped to attention the moment I walked into the seminar room. None of the setup I had ordered had been completed. Instead of one of the smaller banquet rooms I had reserved, our ten tables were located in a dark corner of the giant banquet hall; it looked as if we had expected thousands, but only fifty had signed up. There was no screen to project my slides. The "speaker system" consisted of a single podium with a built-in speaker and attached microphone. The entire arrangement was the exact opposite of what I had specified.

I gasped in horror as I saw plates of cold salad trio already in place at each setting, a full hour before the starting time. Ice melted onto tablecloths, soaking the napkins. Iced tea was diluted beyond any possible taste. Baskets of hot rolls and flavored butter were already on the tables.

My "speaker's table" at the front of the room consisted of one tiny two-top covered by a huge, full-sized tablecloth which dragged the floor, creating a tripping hazard. There was barely enough room for my laptop, much less notes, handouts, props, and water glass.

I turned on my heel and went to find the sales manager, with whom I had so carefully discussed each aspect of the arrangements during a half-dozen face-to-face meetings.

"What in the world is going on?" My question came after the usual cordial greetings, and it was clear her response was already rehearsed.

"I'm so very sorry, Pat, but there was nothing I could do. At the last minute, one of our regular corporate clients needed the room we had reserved for you, and our general manager bumped you to the banquet hall to accommodate him." She shrugged helplessly, hoping I would accept her explanation and be on my way.

I dropped down into one of the chairs in front of her tiny desk and set my briefcase on the floor next to me.

"What do you mean, 'one of your regular corporate clients'? I've contracted for more than a hundred thousand dollars in business with you just in the last year, and have another quarter-million scheduled in the next few months! That doesn't entitle me to some consideration?"

Her face paled as she realized I wasn't going to go quietly. "I know, Pat. You're definitely one of my best accounts, but this is a major national account that books our hotels all over the world, and apparently word came down from corporate that we were to do whatever was necessary to make their meeting happen. I just didn't have any choice."

Stunned, I stared out the window as my mind scrambled for solutions. There was no point in trying to change the hotel's decision; that was a lost cause. The best I could do was negotiate for some immediate changes that would at least mitigate the damages. So, for the next thirty minutes, I directed that the tables be moved out of the corner and into the center of the room where the lighting was brighter. A call to a vendor friend produced the needed screen and audio system, but even he didn't have the lavaliere microphone I needed. All his equipment was out for rental, so I was forced to settle for a heavy handheld mic. The podium and four-top were removed and replaced with a regular clothed banquet table.

But there was no rescuing the sad-looking, tepid meal on the tables. Participants had already begun to arrive as I frantically completed setting up my laptop and projector. I told the sales manager I would speak with her next week about adjusting my bill, and turned to greet my guests.

I excused myself from the luncheon table during the welcome and introductions. In the hallway, I blew my mucus-clogged nose in a futile effort to clear my sinuses enough to breathe. Sweating profusely, I returned to the room and waited at the back through my introduction. " . . . thirty years of experience in human resources management . . . taught thousands of hours of management development training programs . . . adjunct professor at Webster University . . ." Meanwhile, the voice in my head was screaming at me: *What are you doing here? You know you can't do this! Just walk out right now—leave and don't come back!*

In spite of my fear and panic, I made my way to the front, picked up the heavy microphone, and began my presentation. Somehow, I managed to remember my opening story and was gratified by the enthusiastic response, but everything went downhill from there. Disoriented, I told stories out of sequence and ad-libbed transitions, losing momentum and impact. Several times I was forced to put down the mic and turn away to blow my snotty nose. Halfway through, tears of frustration and rage began flowing down my cheeks, dripping mascara-laden tears onto my favorite silk suit.

After what seemed an hour but must have been only minutes, I stumbled through a weak closing, thanked the audience for coming, and apologized again for my illness. I didn't even stay for the normal post-presentation chatting, but left with my tail between my legs.

I was so completely humiliated I doubted I'd ever be able to hold my head up again.

My career was finished.

Chapter 4

I never understood why Mother and Daddy ever got married.

Mother was one of eight surviving girls in a family of eleven children who lived with their parents on a small hardscrabble farm in the country. Poorer than church mice, she often told me, they never had any food they didn't raise in the garden or trade their produce for, but they always managed to have fun. They were in church every time the doors opened and always found some kind of offering to take, usually food from the garden. As soon as she graduated high school, at the age of eighteen, Mother was granted a provisional certificate and began teaching the first through twelfth grades in the one-room schoolhouse at Rose Hill, in rural Haskell County. During the ensuing years, she moved to Miami, Oklahoma, and worked her way through her associate's degree by serving as a live-in nanny and housekeeper for a family of five.

After she accomplished the associate's degree, Mother returned to Haskell County and Rose Hill School, where she taught for several more years. By that time, she had married Daddy and had three babies within two and a half years. I was the youngest.

One of my earliest memories is going to school with Mama when I was only one or two years old.

My brothers were there as well. She couldn't afford to pay a babysitter for us, so we simply became students like the other children she taught. By the time I formally entered the first grade at Stigler, I was reading at the fifth-grade level, and both my brothers were also working above their age levels.

As one of the "men" in his family, Daddy helped his father and brothers work their farm on the other end of Haskell County from where Mother's family lived. Daddy's mother died when he was not yet two years old, and he was raised by his sisters, and step-sisters and step-mother, after Grandpa remarried. They lived poor lives, like all the other farm families in the county. As Daddy told and retold the stories, they were always hungry, and the only thing they ever did was work. He was able to attend school periodically, but in spite of three tries, he never managed to complete the eighth grade. Each time he got close, some family crisis, or a harvest, called him out of school for several weeks at a time.

In spite of his poor education, Daddy was brilliant with numbers. He could calculate addition, multiplication, division and percentages in his head faster than I could ever do on a calculator, and he was never wrong. When he and Mother married, she was twenty-six; he was only twenty.

They shared similar rural backgrounds, but were complete opposites in almost every other way. Daddy had been raised by Grandpa to believe that a man's work was in the field, and a woman's work was in the house. The man was the boss of the household, and the woman was to do as she was told. A devout Christian, Mother did her best to live up to Daddy's standards, but according to him, nothing she ever did was right.

I recall several of Daddy's condescending remarks to my mother.

"What's the matter with you, Willie, don't you know nothin'?"

"That's just stupid, Willie. If you don't know no better'n that, just keep your mouth shut."

"Never seen nobody so stupid with figures!"

"Never mind, you won't do it right noway. Here, I'll do it."

Those were the sounds of my childhood, as Daddy compensated for his lack of formal education by beating Mother down with every word out of his mouth. And by the time I was in the second or third grade, he was treating me the same way.

I wanted nothing more than to please Daddy and to help Mother keep the peace in the home.

Mother always taught school during the academic year and worked as a clerk at the stockyards during the summers when school was not in session. Daddy worked for wages driving a propane delivery truck, or a coal truck. Or he worked on our land, raising and selling beef cattle and hogs for the market, and chickens for the table. Eventually, Daddy become involved in Little Dixie Democratic Party politics, and was elected and served several terms as County Court Clerk.

We were rich by most people's standards. Both Daddy and Mother had full-time jobs and paychecks, plus we raised most of our own food and had occasional income from Daddy's farming ventures. Daddy always bragged that "we may not have any money, but we'll always have food on the table."

And he was right about that. We always had plenty for ourselves, and plenty to share with others.

But Daddy had big dreams and wanted more.

First, he borrowed three hundred dollars from Mother's sister, Aunt Violet, bought eighty acres of land just east of Stigler, and built a small, three-bedroom, one-bath buff brick house with a large kitchen and dining room, huge living room, and three small bedrooms. Heat was from a gas floor furnace, and the floors were oak hardwood that Mother and I refinished every other summer. Furnishings featured a huge living room rug that guests would roll up against a wall when the square dance club came for an evening of dancing. Daddy, of course, was the caller, and he knew the words to every dance and song, which he sang on key and with gusto.

On evenings when the square dances were held elsewhere, Mother paid a young woman to come babysit for us, and we spent hours listening to her read to us from the Childcraft books we loved so much.

But our modest existence wasn't enough for Daddy, and one day in early 1953, we got off the school bus at the house to learn that we were moving to California. Daddy had bought a brand-new 1953 Buick and a new 1953 GMC pick-up, and our belongings were packed and ready to go. We left before dawn the next morning, sleepy but shaking with excitement.

Three long, hard days later, we arrived in a farming community outside Bakersfield, and moved into our first California home. Ours was one of several homes for farm hands that crested a large hill surrounded by alfalfa and cotton fields. Daddy's cousin Harvey was the farm manager, and Daddy drove a tractor plowing and planting the fields.

Life was very different on the farm, but my brothers and I easily adjusted. That summer, the three of us picked cotton in the fields, dragging the heavy sacks between our legs. Daddy had arranged for our pickings to be set aside, so a separate cotton wagon was placed at the end of the field, and rather than emptying our sacks into the same wagon all the other workers used, we emptied ours into "our" wagon. By the end of the picking season, we had filled our wagon almost half full with cotton, and were able to purchase a bicycle with the proceeds.

There was just one problem. The Schwinn Daddy bought was a boy's bicycle, with the large bar between the seat and the handlebars. There was no way I could ride that huge bike; I was still only eight years old. But the boys loved it, and soon were arguing over whose turn it was to ride.

A few months into our stay in California, Daddy had some kind of conflict with Cousin Harvey. Daddy came home at dusk, told all of us to stay in the house, and pulled on a pair of heavy leather gloves, his face grim. He went back outside and as we peeked between closed curtains, we saw the shadowed figures of Daddy and Harvey facing each other. They yelled and circled each other, and then Daddy threw the first blow. A few grunts, clinches, and blows later, Daddy knocked Harvey down. Harvey yelled again, but picked himself up and stalked off. Daddy came back inside with a large, deep, bloody cut on his nose. We moved the next day, without anyone but Daddy ever knowing what caused the fight.

Our next stop was a competing farm a few miles down the road, where Daddy drove farm machinery and we lived in a tiny, two-room cinderblock house for several months, until a horse barn could be modified for our use.

But as soon as he could put together a few dollars, Daddy formed a partnership with another man, Neal Boardman, and together they bought or leased a Mobil Service Station in Bakersfield, at a key intersection on the main highway to Las Vegas. That station was very busy, and patrons frequently paid for their gas with the silver dollar coins they had won in Las Vegas. Daddy began collecting and saving those silver coins, and before we left California, he had amassed several canvas bank bags full of silver dollars.

While Daddy was working at the station in Bakersfield, Mother taught school at Shafter, and we lived in a duplex, part of the converted officer's housing on a former air force base between Bakersfield and Shafter. Our duplex only had two bedrooms, but we were all still young, so the boys and I shared a bedroom with no problems at all.

And what a time we had on that old base! There were miles and miles of sidewalks, and even more miles of abandoned runways. The entire complex was landscaped with acres and acres of meticulously trimmed privet hedges, which provided great cover for late summer evening games of hide-and-seek. There were concrete sidewalks between the lawns and the streets, most of them cracked and heaved up from tree roots, but there was a solid surface, and plenty of shade from the large trees, and I taught myself to roller skate there, on skates that attached to my sandals and were adjusted with a skate key. For hours at a time, I would skate around that housing development, learning to jump over the sidewalk cracks and racing the neighborhood kids. And I frequently came home with bloody knees and hands from the thousands of falls I suffered.

When we dared, a bunch of us kids would leave the housing area and go over to the abandoned runways, where our games were not limited to three-foot-wide sidewalks. There, among the hangers that were beginning to fall into disrepair and the runways whose giant cracks now sprouted with waist-high weeds, we played to our hearts' content until dusk each day.

Mother worked at one of the potato sheds during those California summers. She ran the huge truck scales that weighed the trucks full of potatoes that arrived from the surrounding fields, to be shipped by rail to processing centers. The shed where Mother worked was adjacent to a series of train tracks where loaded freight trains roared by with their cargo many times each day. In spite of the pervasive odor of rotting potatoes, my two brothers and I spent many happy summer days counting the passing train cars, walking the tracks between trains, and learning to forecast the speed and size of the approaching trains by the way the rails were vibrating.

When we returned triumphant to Oklahoma in the summer of 1957, I began the seventh grade. I was twelve years of age, and I didn't know it at the time, but I had already seen the last of my childhood. Those carefree California days of summer would never be duplicated, for in Oklahoma, Daddy was as concerned with status as he was with surviving.

All those bags of silver dollars Daddy had saved bought new furniture. Daddy and mother had a maple, early-American-style bedroom suite, and they bought a dark navy-blue laminated suite for the boys' room. My bedroom suite was the most beautiful though, or at least I thought so. It was made of a blonde laminate, and had a full-size bookcase headboard bed, triple dresser, and large chest of drawers. Once the furniture was in the room, there was barely space to walk between the furniture, but that bedroom quickly became my sanctuary. I spent hours on that bed, propped up against the headboard with pillows, doing homework, or doodling in a notebook, and listening to a New Orleans-based radio station.

The first summer we were back in Oklahoma, we met our new neighbors, who had bought the farm across the highway while we were in California. Mr. and Mrs. Roe and their two boys quickly made us feel right at home again, and my brothers and I began riding horses with the Roe boys. I remember several times when we had watermelon feasts with the Roes in our backyard, and those were fun times. But Daddy wasn't comfortable around Mr. Roe, who was a high school English teacher, so the family gatherings fell away. But the oldest son, George, and I became best friends that summer and passed many a lazy summer afternoon sitting on the tailgate of Daddy's pickup, holding hands and dreaming.

One day Mother came running out of the house, screaming, "Tricia, get in the car! Get in the car! There's a tornado coming!" George dashed across the highway for home, and Mother and I drove the three miles to Grandpa Kelley's house, where there was a storm shelter. As we drove Highway 9 through town, we could see a humongous black wall cloud descending on Stigler, and we were both crying hysterically, literally scared out of our minds, by the time we got to Grandpa's.

Mother and I, and all the other female Kelley relatives, crammed ourselves down into the storm cellar, where we barely noticed the spider webs and mouse droppings. We huddled there for what seemed like hours, listening to the storm scream overhead, and watching the nervous men stand around outside, chain-smoking cigarettes and scanning the clouds. Daddy had never left the court house, where he was again serving as court clerk, and I don't recall where my brothers were, but that storm cellar ritual was as familiar as getting up and brushing my teeth in the morning.

Thankfully, we never experienced a direct hit from a tornado in our little piece of heaven, but there were dozens of near misses. Over the years, tornadoes and hailstorms hit all around us, leaving property destruction, personal injuries, and even death in their wake. But that's just the way things were, and if we were going to live there, we just had to get used to it.

Chapter 5

For a brief time during the summer we returned from California, Daddy owned the old Sigmond Hotel that was located downtown in our small, rural Oklahoma town. He was the only employee and spent his nights in the manager's room near the lobby. My two brothers and I took turns spending the night with him.

I had spent several nights with him before he began molesting me. At first, I loved the closeness, the feeling of being loved, cherished; I thought the petting was a natural extension of our father-daughter relationship. When the petting turned into sexual foreplay, I was repulsed and afraid. Somehow, I felt that what we were doing was wrong, but I was Daddy's dutiful girl and did what I was told.

As time passed and I learned more about what we were doing, I found out in a dramatic way that our activities were not natural at all; in fact, they were quite illegal.

One day in the girl's bathroom at school I overheard two of my classmates whispering. I froze on the toilet, too curious to move. It wasn't unusual for me to do that—to stay back and listen.

The hushed tones sounded familiar to me. "Did you hear that Connie's father was arrested last night? He's in jail!"

A hand flew to my mouth and I stifled a gasp.

"Why? What happened?"

I pictured a hand cupped to the girl's mouth, directing the sound, and strained to hear the even softer whisper. "Momma said he was molesting Connie and her mother caught them."

A cold chill washed over me and I sat there, paralyzed. Suddenly, I knew that if I ever told anyone what Daddy and I had been doing, he would go to jail, and he would kill me for sure. I didn't hate him; I just wanted him to stop.

"Wow!" the girl responded, drying her hands with a paper towel. "I cannot *believe* he's in jail now."

I thought about Connie's dad sitting in a gloomy, damp jail cell, a penitence that could never undo the scars left on his young daughter. And then I pictured my father there, his pleading eyes begging for the sheriff to release him. There was something about that idea—my father rotting in jail—that strangely made me feel somehow safer.

As the girls exited, I stayed put in the now-silent bathroom and tucked this new information away in my heart, stowed it away like a new secret weapon. I knew it would always be available if I ever had to use it.

I thought constantly about that day Daddy claimed one of us had stolen his money from off the piano bench. I thought about him beating me until blood ran down my leg. And I thought about my sobbing mother cleaning me up with her trembling hands.

I never forgave Daddy for that whipping. I never forgot the pleasure he took in it.

Nor did I forgive Mother for failing to protect me. It was not until many years later that I realized how much she had suffered under his verbal abuse, and how that history had rendered her incapable of stopping what he did.

But after that beating, I was no longer a prepubescent adolescent living out the last of her childhood. Every detail of the event remained in my mind where, like a super-slow motion movie, it played out in excruciating, reel-by-reel detail. I would be hoeing the weeds in the garden and suddenly would see Mother standing in the doorway, towel in hand and tears running down her face. Or I would be ironing a pair of denim blue jeans and flash on the expressions on my brothers' shocked faces. Too many times to count, I awoke in the middle of the night feeling again the pain of those savage blows and seeing the expression on Daddy's face in the mirror.

I was obsessed with those memories. Everything I did, said, or thought was a product of those painful times, and for years I lived in fear of another incident. When Daddy was home, I kept track of his every movement, minute by minute, as I plotted ways to stay out of his sight. I became an expert at turning the most mundane chore into a major production so I could stay in the washhouse longer, or take longer to sweep the back porch, or hang laundry on the outside line to dry.

When we were visiting at the home of one of Mother's sisters, the time would always come when Mother would tell me to go outside, or to go watch television in another room, and I would pretend to leave, only to hide and eavesdrop on their whispered conversations. In that way, I learned about the many times Daddy had been seen around the county in the company of some woman, or heard about his latest business project or political deal. Over time, I began to see him not as the omnipotent father who could do no wrong, but as the cheating, conniving manipulator who was both hated and admired throughout the county.

Strangely, I never stopped wanting him simply to love me. Before the whipping, when I would spend the night with him at the hotel, Daddy would spend hours comparing me to his standard of beauty, and I always came up short. He told me matter-of-factly that blondes were prettier than brunettes, and when I got a little older, we would turn me into a blonde. Or he would run his hands over my chest and complain I was too skinny and needed to look more like Nadine, his cousin, Roland's wife, who had a voluptuous figure.

In private, he would tell me my nose was too big, I was too tall, too skinny, too homely, and not pretty enough. And I took all that feedback to heart, believed everything he said, and became self-conscious about my appearance. That self-consciousness turned into shyness and soon became debilitating. I was unable to participate in the group activities of my schoolmates without constantly comparing myself to all the other girls present. It was a brutal way to live, forcing myself to participate in spite of my overwhelming discomfort with my appearance compared to the other girls, and many times I went home after a slumber party, crying about how ugly I was and how no one there liked me for myself, but because Daddy was so powerful in the county.

And as time passed, I became ever more obsessed with exacting some kind of revenge on Daddy. I had been whipped for stealing money I didn't steal? I would steal money! If my brothers were not around, when Daddy hung his clothes on the bedroom door and went in to take a bath, I often took cash from his shirt pocket. Out of a wad of two hundred or more one-hundred-dollar bills, I would take one, then replace the roll. Out of a wad of mixed tens, twenties, and hundreds, I would take a twenty. Even when he had less than a hundred dollars in the pocket, I would take five or ten dollars.

The missing money was never mentioned, so I never knew if Daddy was aware of what I was doing, or never figured it out, or never missed the money. But in my mind, whatever I took was my due for having been whipped for sexual pleasure.

Much later I realized that my "entitlement" behavior was a self-defense mechanism. Each time I did something Daddy had prohibited—smoking cigarettes, drinking beer—I ended up punishing not him, but myself. But I justified all my bad behavior by blaming Daddy for the sexual abuse and whipping. And then I would feel overwhelming anger and guilt because of my own behavior of stealing money from him.

It was during this period that I developed what I later came to call my public persona. I was one person when I was at school, or with a gathering of our large extended family. At those times, I was an outgoing, talented, and confident young woman. But at home, I avoided contact with my mother and brothers for fear I would blurt out one of my secrets. And I avoided contact with Daddy for fear of punishment for some imagined infraction. I seldom spoke at home, and when I did, it was to snap back at Daddy for something he had said to either me or Mother.

Neither persona was comfortable for me. When I was home, I was always afraid. When I was in public, I was always "on," and the stress of those performances took a physical and emotional toll.

Chapter 6

My chance for real revenge against Daddy finally came when I was sixteen years old.

That summer, Mother had finally gotten enough of Daddy's parading around the county with a succession of other women, and filed for divorce. To facilitate the legal action, she and I moved to Muskogee, where he had less influence with the local judges. We spent six miserable, depressing weeks in a rented duplex, crying, feeling sorry for ourselves, and worrying about the future.

One day, Mother decided we should make the forty-five-mile trip home to pick up a few needed things, but she cautioned me that we would quickly get in and out before Daddy knew we were there, so there would be no scene.

As soon as we stopped in the gravel driveway, however, Daddy fishtailed in behind us in his farm truck, spewing gravel and dust everywhere and blocking Mother's car. For the next two hours, Mother and I sat in the airless car while Daddy alternately pleaded, threatened, and begged Mother to "stop this nonsense and come on home." Eventually, both Mother and I needed to use the toilet, so we went inside the house. Mother began scrubbing the filthy kitchen while I used the bathroom.

I puttered and delayed as long as possible, but when I finally left the bathroom, Daddy was waiting and pulled me into a bedroom.

"Patricia, I need you to help me get your mother to come on back home. What can I do to get you to help me?"

I sat on the side of the bed with my head hanging, listening to him beg, and quickly understood that this was my chance for revenge. I let him grovel for a few satisfying minutes while I considered my options, before I finally screwed up my courage, raised my head, and looked him in the eye.

I steadied my voice and in a low whisper, replied, "I'll talk her in to coming home if you'll never touch me again. Ever."

His mouth fell open at my demand, his eyes narrowed as he considered the financial costs of a divorce, versus the personal costs of ending the sexual contact.

Then he finally answered, "I can do that."

I stiffened my shoulders. "I mean it. Never. Ever again. Promise me."

"I promise."

Without another word, I left Daddy in the bedroom and went into the kitchen where Mother was still cleaning.

Daddy had always said, "Women do the housework and us men work outside." The sink and every horizontal surface in the room was piled with plates, bowls, utensils, rotting food (half-finished bowls of breakfast cereal grow rancid quickly), cups and saucers, every glass in the cabinet, and baking bowls I would never have dreamed of using as a serving dish. Layers of cooked-on grease coated every pot and skillet on the countertops.

Mostly, though, Mother was cleaning because it gave her an excuse to avoid eye contact with Daddy. It was impossible to argue with him or to make a point he would listen to while looking at him. He was a master at deflecting every point, countering it with his own arguments, somehow making you feel like a blithering idiot in the process. And he was a far better actor than I ever dreamed of being; when he was lying, his face projected only sincerity and believability.

I picked up a damp towel and wiped the things she had washed.

As I dried, I talked. I gave her every reason I could think of, every excuse for coming home when what we really needed was to go through with that divorce. It took only a few minutes before she began saying things like, "We'd have to go back and get our things," and I knew she was coming around.

I capped my arguments with pleas about how much I would miss my speech and drama activities, and how much I would miss my friends and church if we stayed in Muskogee. Those pleas became the turning point—Mother couldn't *not* do what I asked.

Daddy, of course, had been listening, and as soon as I left, he started in on her again. Every term she wanted, he readily accepted with barely an objection. He promised her the moon, but I knew that at best she'd only get tailings.

But I wasn't thinking about mama at that point; I was thinking about my own deal with the devil, and guilt overwhelmed me as I remembered the gallons of tears she had shed, the years of humiliation she had endured. I also remembered my own beating, sexual abuse, and verbal abuse. The trembling fear I experienced every time we sat down to eat, when I was within reach of his backhand.

Daddy only used that backhand on me one time, when I was particularly frustrated by the dinner table discussion. He had been talking about an upcoming election, and Mother had disagreed with him about her choice of candidates. He spent the next several minutes berating her for her choice, telling her how stupid she was, and talking about what an idiot the candidate was. She was a female, and in Daddy's mind, no female was competent to hold any office, elected or not. Finally, my frustration boiled over and I snapped at him.

"Well, Daddy, that's what you say about all women, except your girlfriends."

He backhanded me so fast I had no time to react, and I ended up on the floor with a bloody nose. And as usual, no one made a comment. I eventually picked myself up, righted my chair, and sat back down.

We all continued with supper as if nothing had happened.

But the memory of that painful backhand stayed with me for years, and I always cowered when Daddy was around.

But my guilt about my deal with the devil would stay with me throughout the remainder of Mother's life, and regret for the pain I caused her has never diminished.

I was already very good at keeping secrets. I had never told a soul about the sexual abuse, or about the whipping. But the cost of that silence was my withdrawal from my family and friends. I spent hours at a time closed in my bedroom, and no longer spent any time at all with my friends Patti, Jackie, or Mary, for fear I would blurt out my awful secrets. I became adept at putting on one face to the outside world while I was cowering inside. I functioned, but suffered on-going panic attacks and severe headaches from the stress.

But the balance of power had shifted in the family, and I now held all the cards. Whatever I wanted was automatically mine. My brothers accused me of being spoiled, and they were right. Mother's unhappiness grew and she became a mere shadow of herself, seldom making any decision without first consulting me. "Tricia, do you think your Daddy …?" she would ask.

True to his promise, Daddy never touched me again, although I continued to live in fear of him.

As I withdrew from personal relationships, I threw myself into doing, and became the go-to girl for anything that needed to be done at school. I was either on stage in the cast or backstage working in every drama production, and prepared at least two entries for every speech contest.

When I was a freshman, I successfully challenged a senior for first chair of the clarinet section in the band, and then became a majorette. In 4-H and later Home Economics, I learned to sew and for years made most of my clothes. By the time I was a senior, I had become the band drum major, and swapped the clarinet for the French horn. I was in church every time the doors opened.

But during those critical years, I never developed the relationship skills so crucial to a successful life, and I was terribly lonely. As I became more and more dependable to the world at large, my emotional stress grew. I was part of every group activity, and was a leader in some, but always felt I was standing on the fringe, in imminent danger of being cast out the moment my secrets became known. With every success in "doing," my guilt about my behavior also grew, and my self-esteem plummeted.

I became two persons in one body.

During my last three years of high school, I became part of a group of girls who called ourselves the Fabulous Five. I always believed I was included in that group because Daddy had made sure the boys and I always had access to transportation. First he bought a used Ford Fairlane for Marvin, and required him to carry Jamey and me to school each day. As soon as Jamey qualified for a driver's license, the Ford became his and Marvin got a newer model used car. When Marvin went off to college, Jamey carried me around, until he left for college, taking the Ford with him. And when I was able to drive I used Mother's car and drove myself, and frequently my friends, on our after-school and weekend excursions.

Suzanne's dad ran the local Pontiac dealership, so Suzanne also had access to a car, and she and I took turns driving and picking everyone up for our adventures. One evening, we drove over to Enterprise, where we illegally purchased a six-pack of beer, then drove back to town, drinking beer and smoking cigarettes. None of us was an experienced beer-drinker, and soon we ended up on the old Lequire Highway, drunk, laughing hysterically, and throwing up out all the car windows. Somehow we made it home safely, but Suzanne was never again allowed to drive us—in her drunken stupor, she had returned the new demonstrator to the showroom covered in vomit. Her father never forgave her. And from that moment on, I was the only designated driver, and was convinced that my transportation was the only reason I was included in the group.

My senior year, when I was seventeen, I was in charge of the annual Home Economics Fashion Show, an event that showcased the senior projects of each of the home economics students. I wrote the script, hounded the other girls to get their garments completed, and worked late into the night finishing my own wool, Vogue-pattern coat. I was also to model in and narrate the show.

Two days before the scheduled assembly, I awoke with a terrible headache and fumbled through my morning routine, disoriented and barely able to see. I swallowed three aspirin on my way out the door, and somehow drove the three miles to school without mishap. But when I parked and turned off the engine, my fingers no longer worked and the keys dropped to the floor. It took some time, and plenty of frustration, but eventually I managed to pick up the keys, gather my books, and make it into the school building.

First period was band for me, but I made it only as far as the first classroom, which happened to be home economics. The teacher saw me come in and immediately told another student to call my father and "tell him it's an emergency!" I remember Daddy herding me outside to his truck through the crowded hallway, his hand an iron clamp on my upper arm, my deeply embarrassed eyes fixed on the floor as I concentrated on staying upright.

I remember nothing else until a little after three o'clock that afternoon, when I awoke. I was lying on the couch at home. One of my friends was asleep in the chair next to me.

"What happened?" I asked groggily.

"Dr. Conklin told your dad you had a nervous breakdown." She called and told Daddy I was awake. He came and took her home, and as usual, we all pretended nothing at all had happened. I never knew what he told Mother about the incident, because she never mentioned it.

Two days later, I emceed the fashion show as if everything was completely normal. The show was a huge hit, and I even modeled the coat I had finished at midnight the previous night. But the experience had reinforced for me that I could be two people; I could fool everyone but myself, and no one but me would ever know.

Chapter 7

I had always dreamed of being a home economics teacher. I had prepared for it my entire life and entered college in the fall of 1962 planning to major in home economics.

But Johnnie Wray changed everything.

When I was fifteen and a freshman in high school, Johnnie was the speech teacher at my high school, and organized a holiday fair around Halloween. The hallways were filled with makeshift booths where teachers and students dressed in costumes and performed magic tricks or sold home-baked cookies and cakes to raise money so the speech team could travel to other schools for contests. Johnnie had dressed as a gypsy and told fortunes for a quarter, and she was remarkably accurate with her prognostications. She told my fortune based on her knowledge of my family, and when she came to my future, she called me "perspicacious" and said I would become a famous public speaker.

At that point, I had no idea what she meant, laughed at the notion, and wondered about her comment with occasional curiosity. But during my senior year in high school, I was surprised to learn that she had awarded me a full-ride scholarship to Eastern Oklahoma State College, where she had been teaching for two years.

I had declared my major as home economics when I was admitted and pre-enrolled, but when I showed up for the start of fall classes in 1962, I learned that not only had I been given a speech scholarship, but I would also major in speech and work a few hours a week in Johnnie's office, where she was head of the speech department. The registration clerk handed me a note that said "Please come see me when you get here." It was signed "J. Wray."

So for the first two years of college, I had tuition scholarships, a work-study program in Johnnie's office that produced a small amount of spending money, and scholarship-provided room and board. I'm sorry and embarrassed to say that, at the time, I really had no idea what Johnnie had done for me, or how that would affect my future. But I blithely entered college as one of the few students whose bills were paid and who did not have to worry about money.

Fortunately, I absolutely loved speech and drama. Every class was easy, Johnnie began coaching me for my speech career, and I had a featured or starring role in every play produced. Under Johnnie's tutelage, I began to envision a different kind of teaching career than I had planned, and home economics was nowhere in the picture.

Johnnie was an amazing coach. She was kind and loving, and delivered her critiques in such a way that I always knew just how wonderful I was, even as we made corrections or changes to my work.

She was married to Lester, a disabled veteran, and they lived in a small rock house a few miles from town. Their place was adjacent to the highway, and

Johnnie and Lester encouraged me to stop by on my way back to school.

They soon became like a favorite aunt and uncle to me, and we spent many Sunday afternoons in lawn chairs under a shade tree, solving the problems of the world. President John Kennedy was assassinated just before Thanksgiving that first year, and together we prayed for his soul and for the future of our country.

My relationship with Johnnie matured and grew more complex over the next two years, but I was the first of her students to realize when, at the age of forty-four, she became pregnant with her first child. She helped me write the original oratory I would take to the Junior College National Tournament, to be held there at Eastern the next year. Once the speech was written to her satisfaction, she coached me on delivery and we practiced for hundreds of hours until I could recite the entire speech in my sleep. The topic was public complacency in the face of great need, and we used the Kitty Genovese incident in New York City for a dramatic opening. Then we wove Bible verses into the script to emphasize our key points. By the time my freshman year was finished, I had already won several regional speech contests with that original oration, and was preparing for the National Tournament.

I was also planning to debate at the National Tournament, and had been working with my colleague, Judy, for several months. But debate hadn't come to me as easily as oration, and while I quickly learned the affirmative role, the negative side completely baffled me. When I was on the negative side, I had to wait for the opposing team's opening statements, contemporaneously prepare arguments against the opposing team's statements, and offer new arguments of my own. This was no pre-prepared oration.

The first time I was to be on the negative team during a practice session, I couldn't think of a single thing to say in spite of several prompts from Johnnie and Judy, and left the room in tears. Fortunately, Johnnie came and found me, gave me a hug, assured me I was better than that, and refused to let me end the day on a failure.

In the end, I won the National Junior College Women's Original Oratory contest with my speech, and Judy and I also won the Women's Debate contest. The tension and stress had been so great that I loudly burst into tears at the conclusion of the last debate, before the results were announced.

My reaction to those accomplishments surprised even me. I was *embarrassed*.

I had always been so lacking in self-esteem that I gave myself no credit for my own work, and told anyone who would listen that the two championship trophies really belonged to Johnnie. When the Honorable Carl Albert, United States Speaker of the House, asked me to speak at his dedication of the new post office in Wilburton, I was overwhelmed and embarrassed. But I managed the speech, and "The Little Giant" was very gracious in his praise. He later had my speech read into the official minutes of the House of Representatives, putting it into the Library of Congress, an incredible honor.

But for years, in my deepest heart, I did not believe I was worthy of all the accolades, because Johnnie practically wrote the speech, and if she hadn't directed my every move, I'd never have won.

Judy had carried our team in the debate contest, and if not for her, we would not have won.

But by that point, when I was twenty, I had become a very good actress and the Pat the world saw was polished and self-confident, while inside I was terrified I would be discovered to be a complete fraud. The duplicity on my part was painful, and I developed a severe case of ulcers. And continued to live that way for the next forty-five years.

Chapter 8

My last two years of college were memorable only for my poor decision-making and my humiliating public failures. The most embarrassing incident happened my junior year, as we were in our second or third performance of that semester's play.

My role was secondary, but pivotal to the plot. The two lead actresses were on stage in the middle of a key scene that set the stage for the rest of the plot. It was a long scene, and the rest of the cast wandered around backstage, waiting for our entry cues.

Doyle stood up, jangled his car keys, and said, "I'm going to Sonic for drinks. Who wants to go?"

"I'll go," I volunteered. I knew I had at least twenty minutes before my entrance; we would easily be back in plenty of time. We took drink orders from everyone and hustled out.

Thirty minutes later, after we had dealt with the usual Friday-night crowds and traffic jams, we made it back with the drinks.

A dozen people grabbed us as we came in the back door. "What happened? You're late! They've been adlibbing forever!"

I calmly set my drink down, pulled on my character's gloves, and stood in the wings to let the girls on stage know I was ready for my entrance.

Inside, I had broken out in a cold, nervous sweat and my heart pounded like a drum.

The cue came immediately. I blithely made my entrance and the play continued as if the entire scenario had been part of the playwright's original concept.

During the rest of the performance, backstage in whispered bits and pieces, I learned the rest of the story. The adlibbing had gone on for more than ten minutes. As soon as she realized I was late for my entrance, the director, Billie Harmon, had come pounding down from the balcony to storm the backstage area, demanding my immediate presence. Of course, I was not there, and neither was Doyle, my cohort. The entire cast and crew were frantic, trying to figure out what they should do if we failed to return. How long should they wait? How would they cover for our absence? What if we'd had an accident? Should they just cancel the production?

Slowly, I began to understand the full import of what I had done. My impulsive decision had created tremendous stress for everyone involved, and I was embarrassed beyond belief.

Before the final curtain had fallen, Billie was backstage again, demanding that I stay after everyone else had left.

"What the *hell* happened?" She was red-faced and trembling; her eyes were two pools of fire shooting daggers straight into my soul. Obviously, she already knew the answer and I did not try to lie.

"We went to Sonic to get drinks for everyone, and they were really snowed under." I shrugged and timidly waited for my well-deserved punishment. I had committed the cardinal sin: I had abandoned a play in mid-production. Me, a drama major on scholarship! How could I have been so stupid?

"That's the most irresponsible thing I've ever witnessed in more than twenty years of teaching drama! Do you have any idea the stress and panic you caused? No, of course you don't, because you didn't think of anyone but yourself!" Turning, she stomped away several steps, tension in every muscle. She pulled heavily on a forbidden cigarette, exhaled loudly, took another deep puff, and turned back to me, smoke drifting up from her nostrils.

"If I had my way, Pat, you'd be immediately expelled from school. But I don't have that authority, so all I can do is report your actions to the department head and let him decide what action to take regarding your scholarship and academic plans. Meanwhile, I can guarantee that you'll never be cast in another play I direct, as long as you're in school here and I'm the drama teacher. Do you understand me?" Unable to make eye contact, I nodded my downcast head.

"Good. Now get out of here. I can't stand the sight of you."

Billie was true to her word for the next three semesters, and I fulfilled my scholarship obligations as a member of the production crews. But she did not cast me again until the final semester of my senior year. I had gone through three miserable tryouts and been humiliated each time a cast list was posted without my name in a leading role, so I was surprised beyond belief when the cast list for "Bell, Book and Candle" showed my name in the leading role.

Then my old lack of self-esteem reared its ugly head again and I began suffering panic attacks.

This is the part Kim Novak played in the movie! Beautiful, blonde Kim Novak, the epitome of Daddy's ideal woman. Why me? No way can I do this!

Somehow I hung in there, learned my lines, and put on a brave face, but inside I was trembling like a leaf in a windstorm from the stress of living two lives. Finally, the stress took its toll and I sent word to Billie that I was ill and wouldn't be at rehearsal. The show was scheduled to open in two weeks.

An hour later, Billie stormed into my dorm room and found me in bed, miserably suffering from a major sinus infection.

"So you really are ill. I wasn't sure this wasn't another one of your stunts." She quickly glanced around and her voice changed from accusation to concern. "Are you taking anything? Can I get you something? Have you seen a doctor? What do you need?"

Tears sprang to my eyes at her kindness after what I had done the previous year. I shook my head at her offer.

"Okay, Pat. Sorry I didn't trust you. Hope you feel better soon." She patted my arm with a gentle hand and left.

And I knew she had just spoken aloud what everyone else had thought: I was untrustworthy.

Just over a week later, the play went on without a hitch and I never missed a cue or a line. But my performance was wooden, and the applause I received was tepid at best.

Later that semester, after failing to receive a single interview for the drama teacher job openings the campus recruiters were trying to fill, I understood that my reputation had preceded me. Without the enthusiastic recommendations of Billie and our department head, there was no way I would be offered a drama teacher position.

But I had minored in English and journalism, and was eventually offered a position as a journalism teacher and yearbook sponsor for a middle school in New Mexico. My last college semester was almost over and I was desperate for a job, so I accepted and walked into another disaster of gigantic proportions.

I was over my head. Way, way over.

Yes, I had minored in English and Journalism, had edited hundreds of student-submitted stories for the college's campus newspaper, and had served as editor for one semester. In addition, I had been on the yearbook staffs in high school and both colleges. But none of that had prepared me for teaching journalism and sponsoring the yearbook.

Beyond that, I'd not had a single class in teaching methods during the four years of my college work. *Lesson plan? What's that?*

But it was the only job I had been offered, so with a heart full of fear I moved to New Mexico to begin my teaching career. Surely I could bluff my way through the first year, until I learned enough to do a good job.

I found a small house to rent and settled in. Two days after I arrived, while I was waiting for my first day at work, rain came in a downpour, and continued monsoon-like, until by the third day, the town was completely flooded. I paced from door to window and back again, watching as the yard filled with water, and when the streets filled, bringing the scant traffic to a standstill, I began to panic. How would I get to work through flooded streets? Would the schools be closed because of the weather emergency? I knew no one in town, had no one to ask about these concerns, and had no idea the school district's history with regard to such issues. So I paced, panic building with every step.

The morning of the fourth day of the rain, I went into the kitchen to make myself a bowl of cereal, only to discover the kitchen was full of ants. Not just a few ants, but columns of them, marching like a marauding army over every surface, in and out of every cabinet, and as I was to discover, colonizing every package of food I had so carefully stocked the day after I arrived.

Raisin Bran? Forget it. Cheerios? No way. Pancakes? Flour ruined. There were even ants in the refrigerator! I called the landlord.

"Well, you must have brought them in with your things," he said, "because that house was completely fumigated before you moved in." His voice was so practiced and nonchalant that he sounded rehearsed. And I knew he had heard these complaints before.

As angry as I had ever been in my life, I struggled to control my voice. "There were no ants in my things, nor in any of the groceries that I bought. This house is uninhabitable and I want to know what you're going to do about it."

He snickered. "I'm not going to do anything about it, lady. That house was clean as a pin before you moved in, so whatever the problem is, it's yours to deal with! Good luck."

I slogged through the rain and high water, bought some spray cans of ant killer, and went to work. Eight hours later, I had swept up trash cans full of dead ants and the place smelled awful, but I went to bed believing the worst was over.

The next morning, there were more ants than ever, and now they were in the dresser, chest, and closet where my clothes were stored. Frantically, I washed and dried everything, checking for ants at every step in the process. By the end of the day, exhausted, and at my wit's end, I called the county extension office for help, only to be told the ants had sought shelter from the unrelenting rain and would disappear as soon as the flood waters receded. There was nothing to do but wait.

I reported to school the next day with huge bags under my burning eyes, and paranoid about possibly having ants in my clothing. During breaks in the orientation, told everyone I met what I had encountered. By noon, the music teacher had offered me a way out.

"I rent this huge house that has a small one-bedroom apartment added onto the back. You're welcome to rent that for two hundred fifty dollars a month if you'd like. Would you like to come see it?" As soon as the workday was over, I went to see the place, and moved in that evening without giving notice to the Antlord.

When the first quarter grades were posted at school, I received an angry visit from the father of one of my Hispanic students. It was during the school's open house for parents. I leaned on my desk and greeted everyone as they entered my classroom and sat at the student desks. They listened as I explained that this class was beginning journalism, and that we spent time learning the basic principles of writing news stories and feature articles. Most importantly, we also produced a weekly newspaper for our school of more than eight hundred students and faculty. Then I asked if there were any questions.

Mr. Martinez sat at a student desk, relaxed, feet extended, with his ankles crossed, the very picture of nonchalance. But his voice was hard and brittle.

"You gave my son an F!" He declared, cocking his head at me. "You can't discriminate against him just because you don't like Hispanics, and I'm filing a formal complaint with the school board." And he smirked at me.

What? He was calling me a racist? I took a deep breath and swallowed my anger. As usual, I pasted a blank expression on my face and tried to convince him otherwise.

"Sir, I did not *give* your son his grade—he earned it, by not turning in a single assignment since the beginning of school. I can't grade assignments I don't receive. I had no choice but to record the F." I crossed my arms and offered a pleasant smile.

He stood and stalked toward me with a pointing finger. "You could have given him an incomplete! You could have helped him with his work. You should have known he has difficulty with English. Why didn't you give him the option of turning in his assignment in Spanish?" He belligerently stood in front of me with his arms crossed over a puffed-out chest.

I felt my first fluttering of fear and forced myself to respond in a calm, measured way. Nausea rose in my throat, and I swallowed it down. I stood to my full height and faced him.

"Sir, I had no way to know your son was having difficulty with English, because he *has not spoken a single word in class* since school started. Nor has he spoken to me in any way, much less asked for help. Has he spoken to a counselor? Does anyone else know how hard English is for him?"

But inside, I had to acknowledge to myself that I had simply ignored the quiet kid who sat by himself on the back row and never spoke to anyone. It was always so much easier to encourage the eager talkers who ate up every assignment and learned new skills as easily as they breathed.

I should have been forcing him to talk to me, asking him what kind of help he needed. But I hadn't, and this scene was the result.

Mr. Martinez paced back and forth in front of my desk and pointed that finger at me. I did what I had always done; I ignored him. I sat down at my desk, picked up my grade book, and began thumbing through it. The longer I ignored him, the more I felt the heat of his anger.

"This is the ninth grade! He's been in school here since he was six years old, and he's passed every class he's ever had, until this one! You're an arrogant, bigoted woman, and by the time I'm finished with the school board, I'll have your job." He put a heavy hand on his son's shoulder and led the boy out the door. He slammed the door behind them with a teeth-rattling bang. I turned and looked with concern at the remaining guests.

The parents sat in shock, silent, abashed.

A voice in the back of the room broke the silence. "She's right," a student said. "He don't never do nothin', not in this class or any other one, either. Mr.

Martinez has a huge chip on his shoulder and thinks the world owes him something because he crossed that river. Well, I don't think that's right." The room exploded with exclamations and comments at the suddenly red-faced boy's response.

I sighed. Thank goodness, it seemed my support was overwhelming.

By the time the principal called me into his office a few days later, I had given careful consideration to the parent's comments and blamed myself for my own failure to approach the failing student and take time to learn his problems. I was still in shock from the rude, hurtful accusations, but was willing to accept my share of blame for poor teaching skills. But I was not a bigot, and would not allow that accusation to stand.

The principal told me in no uncertain terms that I was on probation for the remainder of the year, and if there were any further complaints against me, my contract would not be renewed. In other words, I would be fired. My attempts to explain the nonexistent assignments were cut off with, "Don't waste my time with your excuses! We don't tolerate bigotry or discrimination here, and that's all you need to know."

The situation went from bad to worse. The Martinez boy never turned in an assignment of any kind, and never made an attempt to seek help or to contribute to the group projects. When I tried to speak to him, he smirked at me and turned away, muttering under his breath in Spanish. As soon as the other Hispanics—about sixty percent of the students—saw what was happening, they began missing deadlines and turning in poor-quality work that had to be rewritten or edited by one of the other students. Finally, only a few of the journalism students were turning in assignments at all.

Since we were supposed to be producing and distributing a four-to-six-page newspaper every week, the lack of assignments reduced the paper to two pages, or we were unable to fill even one page and didn't publish at all.

Hispanic students stopped showing up for class, or when they were there, did no work at all but spent their time joking around and disrupting the work of the few who were trying to meet their deadlines.

Each time the paper was published with reduced pages, or with articles filled with grammar and spelling errors and blurry photographs, I would receive another visit from the principal. More than one time, he threw the week's paper in my face and shouted that I had become a laughingstock.

"You get this problem fixed or you won't last the rest of the semester! Am I clear?"

Then the problem spread to the yearbook students, who were missing their deadlines as well, or turning in subpar work.

The day we were scheduled to take the school-wide pictures for the yearbook, I had talked in great detail with the professional photographer who had done this work for the past several years. He had given me a copy of the schedules used the previous two years, and I adapted them as needed, then gave them to the principal for approval three weeks before the scheduled date. Although I had reminded him several times of the approaching date, the principal never responded to my request for comments or approval.

Following the previous years' schedules, the individual photos were scheduled for the morning, by class, and would be followed by the classes, groups, clubs, and teams in the afternoon. Everything was fine through the individual photo sessions, although it was clear there were large numbers of students who were absent and would have to be rescheduled.

But in the afternoon, the principal's secretary failed to make the intercom announcements of which groups were due for their photos, and after three groups in a row failed to show up, I knew I had a serious problem. I asked my friend, the music teacher, what was going on, he went to the secretary to find out, and when he returned, my fears were confirmed.

"He told her not to make any more announcements."

"What? Why? He can't do that!"

"I'm afraid he can, Pat, and he did." We were trying to figure out my next step when an announcement came over the intercom from the principal himself.

"Ladies and gentlemen, the remainder of the yearbook picture schedule has been cancelled. The yearbook sponsor, *Miz* Kelley, has so botched up the schedule that our classes have been completely disrupted, and that cannot be tolerated. We will consider rescheduling the remaining photos for another date, but in the meantime, you are to resume your regular schedules."

The professional photographer was incredulous and ranted about his lost fees and the difficulty of rescheduling around his other contracts. He'd never had such a thing happen, he said, in more than twenty years of fulfilling yearbook contracts. Finally, he calmed down and turned to me.

"Pat, I'm sorry to tell you, but this guy is obviously out to get you for some reason. There's a new journalism teacher here nearly every year, and he puts everybody through the same kinds of hell until they give up and resign. If you need a reference, or need me to speak up for you with the school board, I'll be glad to help. But meanwhile, you should do what you can to protect yourself."

A few days later, the two teachers who occupied the main house, several other single teachers, and I were having cocktails under the shade of a large oak tree in our shared backyard, when someone noticed the principal sitting in his car across the street. He seemed to be taking notes and photographs. We quickly adjourned into the house, and a few minutes later, he left. But he returned several times a week for the next month or so, even on the weekends, until we all felt we were living in a fishbowl.

We pooled our resources and consulted a local attorney, who calmly advised us that the principal had a right to "enforce the provisions of the moral clauses of your contracts." He was not willing to represent us, he said, if we should decide to challenge those clauses, because his children were in the school system, including one in the middle school where we all taught.

By this time, I was a wretched, nervous wreck and had absolutely no confidence in my ability to manage the awful situation to any reasonable conclusion. I was paranoid in the extreme, suffering nightmares and not sleeping, experiencing intermittent bouts of irritable bowel syndrome and horrific headaches, and barely making it through the miserable days. Two weeks before the beginning of the Christmas break, I decided to make one last-ditch effort at saving myself, and requested a meeting with the school superintendent.

I had told no one about my meeting, so perhaps you can imagine my surprise when I showed up and was met by a room full of people. The superintendent was there with his secretary, who, he explained, would be making an official record of the meeting. The principal was there with his attorney. The school district's outside counsel was present. And finally, the district's personnel coordinator was there to "help me understand my rights in this matter."

I was so inexperienced I didn't know that I *did* have rights in the situation, and should have called off the meeting rather than going through with it. But in my ignorance, I sat down and, completely cowed and embarrassed, tried to explain what I had been going through. I was frequently interrupted by the principal or his attorney, who loudly protested every statement I made.

"Absolutely not true! That's a complete exaggeration of what actually happened!"

Then for the next hour, the principal, uninterrupted, detailed a long list of grievances he had against me while I sat completely dumbfounded and unable to make any kind of response. In the end, the superintendent's secretary presented a prepared letter of resignation, which I gladly signed, grateful for the end—any end—to my misery.

Months later, someone told me that the principal had been admitted to a mental institution, and was no longer employed by the school system. Another story I heard was that he had committed suicide. I never had a confirmation of either, but finally began to understand why things had gone so wrong for me, although that understanding was only on the surface. Deep down, the entire semester had been just more confirmation of my own incompetence, and my psyche was badly damaged.

Chapter 9

My resignation was to be effective with the end of the semester, two weeks hence. I ignored that, packed up my things, and headed back to Oklahoma.

And spent the next several weeks trying to figure out what had happened while looking for another job.

Fortunately, the drama teacher at Tulsa Central High School was pregnant, the school was trying to hire a one-semester replacement, and with Johnnie Wray's recommendation, I was hired.

This was a well-established speech and drama program, and the teacher had done a wonderful job of preparing the students for her absence. The main part of my job was place-holding, making sure things didn't fall apart until she returned.

So I monitored the rehearsals for the current play in production, helped the contest students prepare for their forensics contests, and taught the classes, using the lessons the absent teacher had left behind.

It was a routine semester with very little challenge, and I had plenty of time to decide what I wanted to do next. In the end, I decided not to look for another teaching job, and instead applied for a graduate assistantship in the speech department at Oklahoma State University, where I would work toward a master's degree.

I was surprised when I was accepted, but delighted that I didn't have to look for another job. I entered OSU that fall as a graduate student, and immediately assumed my duties.

My first responsibility was teaching the entry-level speech classes, Speech 101. Thousands of students were required to take this class as a prerequisite to any major, so it was taught in two parts. First, in a huge auditorium filled with hundreds of students, the speech professor lectured, explaining the principles of public speaking and making the week's assignments.

Next, I instructed four different sections of labs, during which the lecture students prepared and presented speeches on a variety of topics. I graded their speeches, gave them feedback, and helped them improve their presentations.

But the major part of my responsibility was coaching the freshman debate teams. There were four teams of two students, who researched and prepared for debates on the year's chosen topic. Then they would compete in a series of debates against other college teams at contests around the state.

As their coach, I helped them with their research and critiqued their presentations, just as Johnnie Wray had done for me, until they were ready for the contests. The teams were all very good, and all three two-man teams qualified for the National College Tournament in Brooklyn, New York. As their coach, I was invited to help judge the contests.

OSU had never had teams qualify for nationals before, so they had not budgeted the expenses for the trip, but they paid all our expenses for air fares, hotels, meals, and entry fees. Mother managed to give me a hundred dollars for incidental expenses for the week, and off to New York we all went.

I had never traveled by myself before, but as a judge, I was required to show up two days before the contests began. I arrived at LaGuardia Airport and took a taxi to the hotel. And got the shock of my life when I paid the fare: twenty-six dollars! Plus tip! Suddenly, my hundred dollars looked very meagre.

I checked into the hotel, unpacked my bag in the room and hung up my clothes, and went downstairs to the restaurant for dinner (or supper, as I knew it). I was wearing a dark skirt and white blouse, and looked very nice, I thought. But when I entered the restaurant, the man at the desk just stared at me open-mouthed. When he said nothing, I finally said, "I'd like to have dinner, please."

He puffed out his chest and looked down at me with a hard face. "Madam, we do not seat unaccompanied women in this restaurant."

Now it was my turn to stare uncomprehendingly at him. After a moment, I stammered, "But where will I eat? Is there another restaurant?"

"There are vending machines in the basement. I suggest you try there." With that, he deliberately turned his back on me, leaving me feeling somehow at fault for not having an escort. Then I realized that the patrons sitting closest to the entrance were staring at me with varying degrees of disgust and pity, so I turned on my heel and left.

I returned to the elevator, descended to the basement, and went to the vending machines, where I paid two dollars for a twenty-five-cent package of Lantz peanut butter crackers, and returned to my room.

My room—where the key would not work. I tried several times to get the big brass key to work in the lock, but it just wouldn't, so I went back to the registration desk and told the clerk that my key wouldn't work. He took the key, checked the number, consulted his list, and looked up at me.

"I'm sorry, madam, but there was a mistake in your room assignment and you've been moved to another room. The bellman will escort you there."

A few minutes later, I stared in amazement at the new room. There were two tiny twin beds, and my things had been thrown onto one of the beds. Hanging clothes had been tossed helter-skelter, the make-up case was open and full of items that had been shoved in with no consideration for spillage. Everything was wrinkled, some things had wet spots on them, and I was screaming mad. I left everything as it was and went to find the tournament director at a room down the hall.

She apologized and explained that when my reservation had been made, a regular room had been assigned, but the deal the tournament had made with the hotel required that judges share a room with another judge. *That's what all that stuff on the other bed was—my roommate was already there ahead of me.* I insisted that the director come back to my room with me and see the condition my things had been left in, which she did. She later filed a full complaint with the hotel.

But the incident with the room, and with the downstairs restaurant, convinced me that New York City was as bad a place as I had always heard, and I went to bed that first night afraid of my shadow and what might next happen to me. I never knew if my roommate showed up or not; I never heard the door open or close, and the bed next to mine was not slept in that night.

When I got up the next day, I resolved that I would not waste my trip, so I participated in the morning judges meeting, and then headed off for some sightseeing.

I was afraid of the subway system, because I knew nothing about it, so I bit the bullet and hired a cab to take me into Manhattan.

"Where to, lady?"

"Manhattan, please."

"Where in Manhattan? It's a big place."

I wasn't prepared for that, so I responded with the only name I could quickly dredge up. "Saks Fifth Avenue." He dropped me at the corner of Fifth Avenue and Broadway, I paid another exorbitant fare of nearly thirty dollars, and began my New York adventure.

I paid seven dollars for a tiny, embroidered handkerchief for Mother as thanks for her gift of the hundred dollars, then left Saks as quickly as I could. Next, I walked with the crowds along Fifth Avenue, experiencing the overwhelming noise of the city, and made my way to Tiffany's. There, I feigned nonchalance and browsed the jewelry counters. A clerk following me every step of the way. Finally, I asked, "Where are all the diamonds?" The clerk cocked a haughty eyebrow at me. "Upstairs, of course." She turned away, and I left the store, embarrassed and disappointed.

But the Empire State Building did not disappoint, and I looked through one of the top floor observation telescopes, locating the other places I really wanted to visit. Coney Island, the Staten Island Ferry, and the Statue of Liberty were dimly seen in the mist, and I fixed their locations in my mind and headed out. I walked miles and miles and miles that afternoon—nothing in Manhattan is close to anything else—but saw each of the things I wanted to see.

I ate a hot dog from a cart vendor at Coney Island and took the Staten Island Ferry over to the Statue of Liberty, where I was disappointed to the point of tears with the condition of the statue. It was covered with green mold and pigeon shit, and looked as if no one had cared for it for many, many years. A few years after I was there, a major restoration of the statue was completed, but I only saw it in its worst condition.

In between these visits, I stopped in a public restroom for a toilet break. And was shocked out of my socks when I realized the feet in the stall next to me were in high heels, but pointing backward in the stall! When I exited the stall to wash my hands, there were two very large men, dressed as women, applying lipstick at the lavatories.

I left that place like a scalded cat.

I wanted to experience a traditional New York deli, so I wandered until I found one several blocks away from the ferry terminal and went in. By that time, it was after 4:00 p.m., but the place was packed. People were jammed up next to the meat display case, pointing and shouting at the men behind the counters. I read the menus scrawled on chalk boards behind the clerks, watched a few minutes as other people pushed their way up to the counter, shouted their orders, then retreated with their sandwiches. Finally, I decided the only thing to do was to join the hoards.

I waited for an opportunity, then pushed my way to the front and caught the eye of one of the clerks who, I saw, was making sandwiches as fast as he could work.

He looked at me and demanded, "Whaddya want, lady?"

"Corned beef on rye," I said. "Lightly toasted, with melted cheese and sauerkraut."

"What kind a' mustard?"

"Dijon, please."

"Whatcha gonna drink?"

"Coke, please."

With the speed of light, he made the sandwich, put it in a basket with a pickle and napkin, and shoved it in front of me. "Twelve fifty, lady." Without waiting for a response, he moved to the fountain drink machine, overfilled a cup, and set the dripping mess next to the sandwich. Meanwhile, I was fumbling for money. He'd made another order and taken payment before I finally got my money out and handed it to him. He'd not commented on my fumbling at all; he just moved on.

I found more napkins and snatched a single seat at a tiny table next to the wall, and thoroughly enjoyed the unique taste of my sandwich while I watched the crowd. I quickly realized, however, that every seat in the place was taken and people were impatiently waiting for me to leave so they could sit down with their own sandwiches. Extremely uncomfortable with people staring, willing me to leave, I wolfed the sandwich down and quickly left. I'd been in the deli fewer than twenty minutes.

Somewhere along the way during the afternoon, as I was resting on a bench watching the bustling world go by, I visited with a New Yorker who immediately recognized me as a tourist. Rather than being unfriendly as I expected, however, he was very nice and kindly explained to me in detail exactly how to use the subway system. He said I could ride all over Manhattan and back and forth to Brooklyn for only ten cents a ride! My worries about my money holding out immediately disappeared, and I was able to relax and enjoy the remainder of the trip relatively stress-free.

Early that evening, I bought a first-level balcony ticket to see the hit Broadway show, *Cabaret*! It was a dream come true for a speech and drama major, and could not have been more perfect. Joel Grey and Liza Minnelli were the stars, and I was close enough to the stage that I could have easily reached out and touched them as they belted out their songs. From my vantage point, I was able to watch a lot of the backstage activity, including stage hands moving scenery and props around, players waiting for their entrances, and costumes and makeup being changed or adjusted.

But it was the action on stage that really fascinated me. I had known nothing about the story, only that this production was a huge, Tony-award-winning hit, and I was a great Liza Minnelli fan. So perhaps you can imagine my surprise and delight as I watched, entranced, as a moving drama played out in the background of an exciting, raunchy, funny cabaret show. I'm sure that both Joel and Liza recognized my rapt enjoyment, for they both seemed to play directly to me as they sang key songs or pulled some of the raunchiest of their stunts.

I left the show that night convinced that I would one day direct similarly moving and entertaining productions, and feeling confident with every fiber of my being that I was entirely competent to do so.

I easily took the subway back to Brooklyn late that night, turned right, and walked the two blocks back to the hotel. I called to check on the OSU debate teams, wished them a good night, and went to bed, happy and elated that I'd survived my first day in New York with no mishaps. I'd easily seen what I wanted to see, thoroughly enjoyed my adventure, and hadn't worried for a single minute about whether I was pretty enough or capable enough to meet muster. I was just me, and that was more than enough.

After a challenging but rewarding tournament, my six students and I returned triumphant to OSU with trophies in hand. All three teams had won several debates, and one team had reached the quarterfinals of the contest in our division. Personally, I had never felt more confident or sure of my future path, and was happier than I had ever been.

Then I hit a major obstacle. My thesis advisor, Bunny Locke, wanted me to do my thesis on Harold Pinter, an up-and-coming playwright. I couldn't stand his work, which I thought was nearly pornographic in nature. Bunny saw it as avant gard, and insisted. We were at a complete standstill, and the department head refused to intervene. I either had to research and write the thesis Bunny wanted me to write, or leave school without a degree.

Chapter 10

And then I met Joe Martin, and my life took another dramatic turn.

Joe had just started dating my roommate when I returned from New York, and he was apparently taken by my enthusiasm. Soon he had abandoned my roommate and started taking me out instead, and I fell madly, head-over-heels in love. According to him, he fell in love with me the first time he laid eyes on me.

Joe was thirteen years older than me, divorced, the father of three children who lived in Little Rock with their mother. Originally from New York, Joe had joined the air force and was in his thirteenth year of service. He had qualified for a special program in which the air force was paying for him to complete a bachelor's degree in engineering, after which he would complete the Officer's Candidate School and become an officer. Already a non-commissioned officer, Joe told me that he was a maintenance crew chief on the helicopters that were being sent to Vietnam, and once he became an officer, he would become a battalion commander. I had no idea whether what he was telling me was true, but I was impressed.

A week after we met, Joe asked me to marry him and I immediately said yes. I called Mother and told her we would be getting married at home in two weeks, and somehow she pulled off a miracle and made it happen. She sent out invitations, ordered a cake, rearranged the house for a crowd, and acted as if it were all completely routine. She even managed to arrange for several of my high school and college friends to be there.

There was only one problem.

Daddy refused to give me away, so Mother had arranged for our across-the-highway neighbor, Stanley Holt, to do that. I didn't know about that issue until after Joe and I arrived in Stigler and returned from the court house, where we got our marriage license. The living room was full of waiting guests when we arrived, the preacher was in place, and Daddy was nowhere to be seen. Mother guided me back into the bedroom hallway, where poor, nervous, frightened Stanley was waiting. She explained what was going on and I began crying, but Stanley escorted me into the living room where I cried through the brief ceremony, huge crocodile tears loudly dripping onto the plush carpeting. Daddy showed up sometime during the ceremony and took a seat in the back of the room, then immediately left before the reception. But Joe and I had said our vows and I suffered, red-faced and still crying, through the reception, before we left for our one-night honeymoon at the Camelot Hotel in Tulsa.

The next morning, I put Joe on an airplane to San Antonio for his OCS, and drove back to Stigler, where I would await his completion and return. The school was twelve weeks, he said, and he'd call me with details so I could come for the graduation ceremony.

I passed the twelve weeks working as a checkout clerk in Daddy's Stigler grocery store, and worried constantly about why I wasn't hearing from Joe. Not a letter, a postcard, or a telephone call. And the twelve weeks passed without word about the graduation ceremony. By this time I was truly worried, and angry, about why I had been abandoned by my new husband, so when he finally called sixteen weeks after he left, I was so relieved to hear from him that I didn't even ask him what had happened. He was already on station at Rantoul Air Force Base south of Chicago, Illinois, had moved into our assigned officer housing, and was waiting for me to arrive.

"Where've you been?" he wanted to know. "I expected you to be here when I got here."

I packed my car, left the next day, and arrived at Rantoul after a grueling thirteen-hour drive. By that time, we had been married more than five months but had spent only one night together, and I was nervous but excited to begin our married life together.

But the Joe I found was not the same man I had married. Not the happy, optimistic man I had met and dated, Joe was now moody and uncommunicative. He worked long days, from 7:00 a.m. to after 6:00 p.m., and when he came home, he was always in a bad mood. He sometimes ate whatever I had prepared, but sometimes not, then sat down in front of the television, where he stayed until bedtime. When we retired for the night, sometimes he wanted sex, but usually not; when we did have sex, there was no foreplay, only a quick, painful penetration, then release for him and out, and sleep, with barely a grunt in between. I was not a virgin when we married, but had so little experience with sex that I had no idea what to do, or even if what we were doing was normal or not.

I only knew that I was extremely unhappy with the way things were, and after only a few weeks, I decided I needed a job. I was terribly lonely during the day while he was at work, knew no one else on the base, and though I had knocked on several doors in our unit, no one had answered and no one had welcomed me there in any way. I was too late to find a teaching job—by then it was approaching Thanksgiving. So I looked in the newspapers and learned that the Magnavox plant in Champaign-Urbana, about twenty miles south of the base, was expanding to meet the war demands and needed to add another shift of workers.

At that point, I didn't care what Joe thought, and applied the next day. After a brief interview, I was hired for the second shift and would work from three o'clock in the afternoon to midnight, six days a week. But first, I would be trained on the midnight shift, midnight to 6:00 a.m., for a week. I was to be an assembler.

That evening I told Joe what I had done.

"What took you so long?" was his only comment. I was heartbroken; I'd hoped he'd be proud of me for contributing to the household income, or at the very least ask what I'd be doing. Instead, he had absolutely no interest whatsoever in what I was doing. We were strangers, and we had only been married six months.

But I began working at Magnavox, and absolutely loved it. The training was fascinating, and it was easy for me. With all my previous sewing experience, it was easy for me to learn to read the complicated blueprints—they were no worse than the sewing patterns I had mastered years ago. The assembly was a snap as soon as I learned to identify the various parts, and learning to solder felt like putting on a comfortable old coat. I finished the week's training at the top of the class.

When I reported for work on the second shift, I was assigned to work on an established assembly line between two "old hands" who had been there for years. They were to "show me the ropes" and "keep me in line," according to the supervisor, who had himself been on the line for years. We were assembling the radios that went into the helicopters destined for Vietnam, and in my mind, I was helping Joe in his maintenance crew chief job.

But within a week, I was bored out of my mind. The assembler on my right, Wanda, assembled her part of the radio, then pushed it over to me. I added my parts, then pushed the radio on to the assembler on my left. But before I was able to do my work, I had to wait for Wanda to do hers, and she was slow. We were in the middle of the long assembly line, and the workers had established their routines over the years. They worked at a set rate, which was excruciatingly slow, and they never varied from that rate.

While they worked, they gossiped. They talked about their husbands, and the sex they were getting, or not getting, in great detail. Their daughters were all sluts, their sons were all geniuses, and their daughters-in-law were all lazy and stupid. Their grandchildren, of course, could do no wrong and were all cute and adorable as they could be. I had absolutely nothing in common with any of them, and any attempt I made to inject anything new into the conversation was met with a brief silence, before they returned to their gossip.

They also talked about the plant—their coworkers, their supervisors, the quality inspectors, the plant managers—and everyone came up short of their expectations. It was, in short, a negative, discouraging atmosphere and I hated it.

But I did love the work. I felt a tremendous sense of accomplishment every time I completed a radio and passed it on, and soon became adept at identifying faulty or flawed parts and discarding them before they could be used. I hated the waiting between radios, however, and began to set goals in my own mind. *I completed six assemblies last hour; I bet I can complete seven in the next hour.* The only problem was that I had to wait for Wanda to supply me with her finished work before I could do my own.

I began to tease her that we could do more with just a little more effort, and soon we had a bet with the entire line that we could do ten units an hour. And we did! And then we did twelve per hour, and then fourteen. Within two weeks, we had more than doubled our line's production, setting all kinds of productivity records and earning the attention of a grateful plant management team.

As soon as the ladies realized they really could do more, however, they became suspicious that I was "a management plant", there to increase production beyond what the union had agreed to do. I was shocked, and vehemently denied their accusations, but to no avail, and soon we were back to six units an hour and I was once again bored out of my mind. Only now, I was also ostracized by everyone on my assembly line and had no one to take my breaks with. As soon as I sat down at a table, everyone there got up and left. Or if I asked if I could join a group, I was told they were saving the seat for someone who was in the restroom.

My non-relationship with Joe had already taken a huge toll on my fragile self-esteem, and I descended into full-blown depression. I blamed myself for making a major mistake in not waiting, learning more about the plant workings, before trying to change things, and one day I went and talked with the personnel manager who had hired me.

"Oh, Pat, I'm so sorry you're having such a hard time," she said. "I was afraid that might happen as soon as I heard about the goal-setting bets, but I really hate that it did."

We talked for a long time about the plant culture, and how one had to go along to get along. And we also talked about her frustration in dealing with the tough steelworkers union, who seemed to believe that their job was to prevent any improvement in plant methods or productivity, at any cost.

But she was very encouraging in the end. "You've already built a great reputation here, Pat. Did you know that you have a perfect quality record, and that's never been achieved by any other assembler in the history of this plant?"

I was stunned. I hadn't known that. All I knew about my quality was that I'd never received a visit from one of the quality inspectors. I just assumed it was because they'd never checked my work. But that was not the case. In fact, the personnel manager told me, all the managers and supervisors in the plant had been told to find out how I had managed such perfect quality, and my name was constantly on the lips of the management team. In a *good* way.

I left the personnel office in a much improved mood, determined to learn how to get along with these older, more experienced women, no matter what it would take. That same week, however, a new quality inspector job opened up, and three different managers approached me, asking me to sign up for the job. When Wanda overheard one of those conversations, she flatly told me to sign up, because I was never going to make it on this assembly line. I heard the implied threat in her voice and words, and signed up that day.

I began the quality inspector job the next week, and said goodbye to the assembly line with only a few regrets. The new job turned out to be only slightly less boring than the old one, however. Working in a clean room with other inspectors, I attached the finished radios to an electronic testing machine, ran a report, and if the radio failed any aspect of its performance, I tagged it and set it aside to be returned to the line for repairs. At the end of each shift, I compiled a report detailing the failures, and the operators who had made the mistakes, and put it in a box on our supervisor's desk. He consolidated the various inspector reports into a management report and sent it upstairs to the bosses. The flawed radios were returned to the line for repairs.

But soon I began to realize that many of the flaws were so minor that I could correct them at my inspection station and send the radio on for shipment, rather than sending it back for repair. That made the job much more interesting, but once again was outside the operating guidelines set up by the union, so I was admonished not to do that in the future.

"Why?" I asked.

"That's not the way we do things here," was the response I got. More frustration.

In my spare time, I used my college research skills and conducted a quiet study, then compiled a report for management. The study revealed that incorporating the minor repair tasks into the inspector job duties would increase productivity by more than twenty-two percent, allowing the plant to ship significantly more finished radios to the front lines. I sent the report to the plant manager, and just over a week later, he called me into his office.

"Pat, I'm really impressed with your work on this report," he said. "And I want to thank you for doing it. Did you work overtime to get it done?"

"No sir, I did it along with my regular inspection duties. The pace is pretty slow out there, as you know, so there was plenty of time. Do you think the findings are valid?"

"Oh, no doubt about that. In fact, I have a bunch of engineers with egg all over their faces because they hadn't already done this study. How'd you learn to do things like that?"

We talked at length about my college background in debate, and how I learned to anticipate opposing arguments. We talked about some of my college research papers, and those results. And finally, he asked me if I would be willing to review the study with the engineering team and teach them how to do similar studies.

But I demurred. Once again my poor self-esteem got the best of me, and I believed there was no way I had anything to teach a group of graduate engineers. The plant manager told me that if I changed my mind, which he hoped I would, he'd help me get started right away.

I returned to my station in the quality lab both encouraged and depressed. I was thrilled with the confidence the plant manager had shown in me, but depressed that I didn't have the confidence to take advantage of what was an obvious opportunity.

As I thought about it during my drive home that evening, I sadly recalled many other times when I had allowed my poor self-esteem to hold me back, and remembered all the times Johnnie Wray had lovingly told me that I could do whatever I made up my mind to do. "All you have to do is believe in yourself the way I believe in you," she had said, over and over again. Now I finally understood what she had been trying to tell me, and by the time I reached the duplex I shared with Joe, I had resolved to do whatever was necessary to eliminate my lack of belief in myself.

Chapter 11

That was easier said than done, however. As soon as I started working the second shift, Joe had told me his work schedule had changed and he would be going on a series of temporary weekend assignments, helping troubleshoot problems at other bases where the Vietnam helicopters were being maintained. Of course, I had no reason not to believe him, but now we were spending even more time apart. He was asleep when I arrived home from work about one o'clock in the morning, and gone when I woke up between 8:00 and 9:00 a.m. Now he left after his shift on Friday evening, and didn't return until late Sunday evening after I had already started my new workweek. We spoke in passing only one or two times a week, if that.

When we did speak, we both expressed frustration with our conflicting schedules, but assured each other that the situation was temporary and we would survive. But as the weeks wore on, I became more and more lonely, and badly needed an outlet of some kind besides work.

One Saturday afternoon, I ran into Lieutenant Walters, one of Joe's coworkers, and his wife at the Base Exchange, where we were all stocking up on groceries and supplies.

"Hey," I said, surprised to see them, "how'd you escape the temporary assignment this weekend?"

He immediately looked at his wife, who raised her eyebrows at him and nodded sideways at me. "Tell her," she said.

"Shit." Looking about as uncomfortable as I've ever seen anyone look, Walters's shoulders slumped and he began tugging on his sleeve. "Look, Pat, I'm really sorry to be the one to tell you this, but there is no temporary assignment. Never has been. Joe's been taking a dead-head back to New Mexico to spend time with one of his ex-wives. He's been bragging about it, talking about how naïve you are and how you'll never suspect. I'm really sorry."

My breath failed me and I stiffened, but as I carefully examined his face, I knew he was telling the truth. "How long has this had been going on?" I asked, in a trembling voice.

"Ever since those so-called temporary assignments started. There's no such thing, never has been."

Now I was even more shocked and immediately asked, "You said 'one of his ex-wives.' How many ex-wives are there?"

"Hmmm. Four, that I know of."

That was enough for me. I left my basket where it was, left the Base Exchange, and went back to our duplex to lick my wounds and decide what I should do.

Early Sunday morning, while I was still holding ice on my swollen eyes, Tiffany Walters called and asked if she could come over. I put the coffee pot on and was dressed by the time she arrived.

She wasted no time with small talk.

"Tracy and I talked last night about your situation, and I decided you need to know the rest of it," she said. "Are you ready for the bad news?"

"How much worse can it get? Let me have it." Inside, my stomach was clenching and I hoped I wasn't about to throw up.

"Here's the thing," she began. "Tracy and I think you need to go talk to someone in the Adjutant General's office about your situation. They're the legal arm of the air force, you know." I nodded and she continued.

"They have a file full of stuff on your husband, and they've had it for years. Anyone who's been around any time at all knows all about him. Everything we know is unofficial, but the gossip is that he has already been warned several times about his immoral behavior, and he was busted in rank at least once because of it. I don't know how long you knew him, or what he told you before you got married, but we know for a fact that he's been married at least four times before you, and he has several kids. We couldn't believe he got into that college degree program after all the problems he's had, but apparently some general wanted to get him out of his command and that's the way he did it." She paused and looked carefully at me before going on.

"Pat, did you think it was strange that you didn't go with him to OCS, or at least come to his graduation?"

"Yes, but I didn't know the protocol in those situations."

"Well, the truth is that at least half the people there brought their spouses with them, including Joe Martin! There was a woman there with him the entire time, and he introduced her to everyone as his wife. That's why we've been so standoffish with you since you got here; we didn't know if you really were his wife or not, or who that other woman was, until he started bragging about his weekend excursions.

"Listen, Pat, several people have already complained to the base commander about Joe's behavior, and we believe he's about to face a court martial for conduct unbecoming an officer, or something like that. I really have no idea whether that will happen or not, but . . . we just thought you should know."

If I decided to go to the Adjutant General, Tiffany said, I should not tell them that Tracy and she had spoken to me. It was considered a breach of ethics for one officer to gossip about another. But if I did decide to go, there were several things I needed to know. And she spent the next half-hour dictating a list of things I should ask to see in Joe's personnel file. As his declared spouse, she said, I had the right to see those things, and I should insist.

By the time she had finished her list, it was nearly noon, and Tiffany had become increasingly nervous about being there when Joe got home. She left after begging me to "keep me and Tracy out of this."

I simply didn't know what to do. I was confused; my mind wouldn't work logically no matter how hard I tried to corral those damaging thoughts that kept cropping up. *I was too ugly. I was stupid to ever have fallen for his shtick. In love with me? Hah! He was no more in love with me than pigs could fly! Why would he be? I was a stupid, ignorant hick who was so lacking in self-esteem that I fell for the first guy who showed any serious interest in me. What a fool I was! Daddy was right all along.*

By the time I had gotten control of myself enough to begin making a plan, Joe was home and all I could do was revert to my public persona and pretend everything was normal. It was the most miserable evening of my life, and I thought it would never end.

I went back to work as if nothing had happened, but while I worked, my mind never stopped. I could do this, I could do that. What if this, or that? Every possible horrible scenario made its way through my mind at one time or another during the day, and some twice, until by the end of my shift I was a nervous wreck and barely able to drive home.

But the moment Joe left for work the next morning, I began a search, and found dozens of love letters he had received from five different women over the past several years. One name I recognized as that of his last ex-wife, and another I realized was the mother of his three children who lived in Little Rock. I tucked those letters away in case I needed evidence of some kind.

I woke the next morning with a terrible sinus infection and called in to work, to let them know I wouldn't be coming in. And then I got dressed and went over to the Adjutant General's office, and asked to see an attorney. Sometime later, I was shown into the office of a very nice young man who appeared to be about my age, and I explained my problems and asked to see Joe's file. He looked more and more uncomfortable as I spoke, and then was quiet for some minutes as he gazed out his office window. Finally, he looked back at me.

"Mrs. Martin, I'm very sorry to tell you this, but whoever told you that you could see your husband's file was mistaken. Those files are completely private, and available only to the commanding officers and the legal office. I will tell you I am familiar with your husband; his name is well-known around here. And I do want to help you, but I just can't. Legally, there's not a single thing I can do for you. However . . ." He paused and reached into a lower desk drawer and came out with a huge file that was at least six inches thick. "I do have a meeting I need to go to, and it shouldn't take more than two or three hours, so I invite you to stay here in my office and make yourself comfortable until I get back. Just take your time, okay?" While he was talking, he turned the file to face me and I saw Joe's name across the top. On top of the file, he placed a clean legal pad and pen. "Do you have any questions for me before I go to my meeting?"

I told him no, and thanked him for all his help, and he left, closing the door behind him. I was alone in his office, and the blinds were closed. I moved over to his desk chair, opened the file, and started making notes.

More than two hours later, I left, armed with more than enough information to make a case for divorce with no problem at all. I tucked the legal pad under my arm and thanked the corpsman on duty as I exited the office.

That evening when Joe got home from work, he was surprised to find me there and I explained that I had called in sick. I then confronted him with what I had learned.

And then he surprised me. He confessed that he had lied to me all along, because, he said, he loved me so much he just had to have me in his life. He confessed that his weekend junkets had been because his ex-wife "needed" him, and he just hadn't been able to sever the tie. He begged me to stay with him and give him another chance, because, he admitted, the air force had already threatened a bad conduct discharge if he ever divorced again.

There were just enough truths among the lies that I believed much of what he said. Everything except how much he loved me. I was too hurt to believe that. But I pretended to believe him, and we went to bed with him believing that I had bought his story and would stay with him.

But I didn't believe his sincerity at all.

My only question was how to get away from him safely and with as little drama as possible. As soon as he left for work the next morning, I packed my sewing machine and clothing into my car and headed south.

I spent the next two weeks listening to Daddy repeatedly tell me, "I told you so!" until I was almost insane. When Daddy wasn't yelling at me, I was on the telephone with Joe, listening to him beg me to reconsider and come home. Finally, Joe came to Stigler and made one last attempt to talk me out of a divorce so he could save his career. Instead, we eventually decided on a no-fault divorce and hired an attorney in Muskogee, whom Joe agreed to pay. Joe said he had received orders for Vietnam and was on his way to San Francisco, where he would ship out in the next week. The divorce papers were prepared, the divorce was filed in Haskell County, where Daddy still knew the judge, and Joe left for California.

A few days later, I swore before a Haskell County judge that there were irreconcilable differences in the marriage, and the divorce was granted, just a few days short of nine months after we had been married.

Chapter 12

I spent only a few days licking my wounds, but in general had already begun to feel better about myself just for having made a decision and taken action. I was proud of myself for no longer being taken advantage of, and for standing up for myself.

Badly needing a job, I called one of my high school Fabulous Five girlfriends for help. Sharon and her husband, Jimmy, lived in Tulsa, where both were teaching school. I briefly told Sharon what had happened and asked if I could stay with her and Jimmy while I looked for a job. She said, "Tricia, you're an answer to prayer. Jimmy and I are leaving tomorrow for Wyoming to work in a national park this summer, and we've worried about leaving our house empty all summer. Why don't you come live here this summer, rent-free, and take care of the house for us? You won't even have to pay the utilities—we've paid them up in advance."

Oh, my Lord, talk about an answer to a prayer! I had no money to make a rent deposit, and had no idea how I would have found a place to live in Tulsa. But there was sure no work to be had in Stigler, and Tulsa had seemed like the best option from the beginning. This offer was a miracle, and I quickly accepted. The next day, I drove to Sharon's home in Tulsa, where she showed me around and gave me the keys, and then she and Jimmy immediately left for Wyoming.

I bought a newspaper, and saw an ad that said Telex was hiring for summer replacement help. I knew that Telex was a United Steelworkers plant, so I went out and applied, and was hired on the spot. Once again I would be an assembler, and would be making enough money to sustain me until I could find a teaching job for the fall semester.

I cried with relief on my way back to my summer home, and set about thanking Sharon and Jimmy any way I could, by cleaning their house from top to bottom. It was not dirty by any means, but it had been lived in and showed it, especially in the kitchen. Over the course of the next few months, I scrubbed every inch of the kitchen, including the pots and pans. The bottom of each one was coated with several years of accumulated oil and grease, and I went through several boxes of SOS pads until every pan sparkled like new. I knew they would never accept any kind of monetary payment, so I made the best offering I could and hoped it would be enough.

At Telex, I was fortunate to be assigned to the day shift, went to work at seven o'clock each morning and was home by three-thirty each afternoon. Without the need for any training, I read blueprints, chose parts, and assembled the control panels on those huge computers they made in those days. The work was easy, I kept my mouth shut, did the work, and went home at the end of each shift feeling that I had done good work.

Financially, the first few weeks were tough. I'd arrived in Tulsa with only about forty dollars in my purse, and there was no way I was asking Daddy for any money. So that forty dollars had to last until I got a paycheck, three weeks hence. I bought a few sandwich makings for my lunch sandwiches, and bought gas for the car, and the forty dollars was gone. I had found a frozen package of hot dogs in Sharon's freezer, and for the last ten days before I got paid, I existed on one hot dog a day, thankful I had at least that. Once again, Sharon had come to my rescue.

When I wasn't at work, I was calling everyone I knew, asking if they knew of any speech and drama teaching jobs. One day, quite out of the blue, I received a call from the principal at Sand Springs High School, just west of Tulsa. He told me his current speech and drama teacher had just been drafted and was on his way to Vietnam, and Johnnie Wray had told him I might be available. Would I come interview?

Would I! Two days later as arranged, I drove to Sand Springs after I got off work, and was hired immediately, to start work in late August. Once again, another miracle! My starting pay would be $7,500 for nine months' work, more than I'd ever made in my life, and I was sure I was about to be rich.

I gave notice at Telex. They were not surprised; I had told them when I was hired that I hoped to find a teaching job after my work with them ended. They enthusiastically told me congratulations and encouraged me to come back each summer as long as they had work. I continued working there until mid-August, and then moved to Sand Springs just in time to start the fall 1969 school year.

As I said earlier, I had always attended church and did have a strong faith in God, but I had not lived the life of a Christian and had not attended church for more than two years. However, I was convinced that I was the recipient of God's grace, and that He had been looking out for me, just waiting for me to get out of my own way and renew my faith in Him. I felt so overwhelmingly thankful, the first thing I did after moving into a rent house in Sand Springs was join the First Baptist Church. The next thing I did was make a trip down to Wilburton to tell Johnnie thanks for all her help over the years, and for her enduring patience with me as I disappointed her over and over again.

She, of course, denied that I had ever disappointed her in any way, told me how much she loved me, and sent me back to Sand Springs with a song in my heart.

Soon, however, I began receiving credit card bills in my name, some with balances due over $25,000. A few telephone calls later and the details were clear. Joe had used the cards liberally on his way to California. He had bought dozens of sets of tires. Stereo sets. Furniture. Expensive clothing. Jewelry.

All things he could sell or pawn as soon as he reached the West Coast.

Once again, I had to deal with the humiliation of my own poor decision-making, and with the embarrassment of being in extravagant debt. I begged for mercy, and two of the cards forgave their debts completely. But I spent the next several years paying off Mobile Oil and Texaco, to the tune of five dollars a month each, until I had paid more than twenty-five thousand dollars for debt that was never mine to begin with.

Chapter 13

I was in my first year of teaching speech and drama at Sand Springs High School near Tulsa, where there was a great tradition of fabulous stage productions and bringing home trophies from forensics contests.

That first year, still high on my own God-given good fortune, I optimistically decided that we would participate in the state's upcoming semi-centennial celebration by staging Rodgers and Hammerstein's fabulous *Oklahoma!* Clearly I was quite insane, but I asked the music teacher, RT Shields, to be the production's musical director and hHe agreed. Together we held tryouts, and ended up naming two complete casts for the major parts. What talent we had!

As soon as I announced the production, an excited buzz spread to the entire school and then the community. The buzz grew to a dull roar when I announced the cast, which included two star football players, the homecoming queen, and three popular student council officers. Everywhere I went, I was greeted with enthusiastic comments from parents, students, faculty, and prominent members of the community. The local newspaper wrote several glowing feature articles about the production, my background, and the cast.

And the more the publicity, excitement, and expectations grew, and the more euphoria with which I had started the year, the more I questioned myself. *Why on earth did I think for a moment that I could possibly pull off such a massive venture? I had absolutely no experience with musicals. Had never staged dances or fights. Had never worked with such a large cast. Had never managed such a complicated rehearsal schedule.* My fear of failure became almost overwhelming, even while I was pretending complete confidence to my students.

Fortunately, the normal production problems kept me functioning. The more popular students didn't take their responsibilities seriously in the beginning, and I had to become quite firm with them to keep them moving. Some cast members had difficulty finding the money to purchase materials to make their costumes, and I found donations for some, and sewed several of the costumes myself, working long into the night more than once to get them finished.

But the biggest crisis came just hours before the scheduled opening.

Walter, a third-year senior who had only been able to memorize his lines with the help of his sophomore girlfriend Angie, waited until everyone else had gone home after our final dress rehearsal, and finally came to tell me that he couldn't go on tomorrow.

"I just cain't do it, Miz K."

Walter had been cast as Ali Hakim, the womanizing itinerant peddler and comic relief for the play. The show could not proceed without him.

Quaking inside, I led him to a seat in the dark auditorium and sat with him while he told me of his fear.

"I ain't nothin' but a joke around here," he said sadly. "I cain't read. It took me three times to pass enough classes to be a senior, an' I wouldn't 'a got that far if it wadn't for Robbie doin' most'a my work for me. Ever'body else in my class already graduated three years ago, so ever'body knows how dumb I am, an' I ain't even gonna have enough credits to graduate this year. There ain't no way I can get up there on purpose an' listen to them hollerin' and makin' fun of me. I just cain't do it."

We sat in silence a few minutes while I gathered my wits, my hand on his forearm for comfort. I began by acknowledging his fear.

"And whether or not you graduate this year, you'll be drafted and sent to Vietnam."

"Yeah."

Then I channeled Johnnie Wray and told him, "Well, I believe this play is your opportunity to turn your life around, Walter, and to become the man I know you are."

I reminded him how hard he had worked to memorize lines he couldn't read, and how perfect he was for the part. His entire life, Walter had covered his illiteracy with jokes and class clown behavior. As a result, his comedic timing was flawless and I knew the character would be the hit of the show. I reminded him how hard the entire cast and crew had worked and how disappointed they would all be if the show were cancelled. I talked about costs, and how much money and sweat everyone had invested in staging the show. I talked about the school's reputation for always having outstanding productions. And I told him that if he didn't go on as planned, he would only be confirming everyone's opinion that he was nothing but a laughing-stock.

"You're better than that, Walter," I told him, and I really believed that. "And you can leave that old Walter behind if you make the right decision for yourself. I believe in you, and know you can do this. And I also know that if you do go on, it will be the turning point in your life."

Finally he left, saying, "I just don't know, Miz K. I'll think about it, but I just don't think I can do it."

Somehow, though, Walter found the courage to show up, and fulfilled his role with stunning perfection. Where he had expected jeers and catcalls when he walked on stage, he received laughs and standing ovations. He remembered every line, every prompt. His comedic timing was amazing. At the close of every performance, he received long, enthusiastic cheers along with the standing ovations. He was the star of the show and the center of attention in school, and his self-esteem would never be the same. And, by the way, he graduated high school the following spring.

A magical year followed our success with *Oklahoma!* I staged three more plays, two comedies, and a drama, all to sold-out audiences and rave reviews. My speech and debate teams participated in fourteen contests and brought home arms full of trophies from every contest. I was flushed with success after the best year of my life, and as a result, my self-esteem had never been higher.

Since my salary as a teacher did not include the summer months, I needed income and worked as a replacement typist at National Tank Company, a local manufacturer just up the road from Sand Springs. My work was in the engineering department, where I typed complex, multi-copy forms on an old manual Remington typewriter. My speed and accuracy impressed the engineers and soon I was offered a full-time job. The personnel manager told me that if I ever decided to stop teaching, I should call him.

"I'll hire you in a New York minute," he said.

That fall, RT and I decided to stage *Carousel*, another Rodgers and Hammerstein hit, and we were just six weeks away from opening when my mother was murdered.

And there was only one suspect.

Chapter 14

I arrived home from school after a rough rehearsal Monday evening, and found my neighbor, Stanley Holt, waiting for me. Stanley was the man who gave me away at my wedding, when Daddy refused to have anything to do with it.

Stanley told me that Mother had died, and he had come to take me home to Stigler.

"What? How? When?" Somehow, what Stanley said had made no sense at all. Mother was only fifty-six; she had been depressed but otherwise not at all ill.

"Did she have a wreck? Did she fall?" I asked question after question that Stanley carefully deflected with, "I don't really know the details, honey. You'll find out when we get home."

I called my principal and my preacher, Brother Bill. The principal told me to take whatever time I needed. Brother Bill was there within five minutes to pray with me. And then Stanley delivered me, sobbing, to Stigler.

He took me to Aunt Violet's home, rather than taking me to Mother's house. One of Mother's seven sisters, Aunt Violet, was terminally ill with cancer, and when I walked in, she sat straight up in her bed and said, "He finally did it, Tricia. He killed her!"

Aunt Dorothy held Violet, saying, "Hush now, Violet, you don't know that." We were all crying, grieving, and hugging each other. I was trying to get answers, but everyone talked at once, voices overlapping like the chirps of birds at the feeder, stories fragmented and varying wildly from person to person. The house was packed with relatives and friends, everyone trying to make sense of what had happened. It was impossible to have a quiet, private conversation because every person there believed he or she had a right to hear every detail, every rumor, and every speculation about what had happened. Like the chorus in one of Shakespeare's plays, every comment was marked with oohs and aahs of surprise or consternation. Aunt Oma finally shooed everyone out of Violet's bedroom except me, herself, Dorothy, and Violet, and they told me what they knew, and what they thought they knew.

Mother had not shown up for work that morning, and her principal and brother-in-law, Buddy Hill, had first tried to call Mother, then called his wife Dorothy, mother's sister, and asked her to go check on Willie. Dorothy's boss at Hayes and Buchanan mercantile, Eulis LaFave, drove her out to the house, where they found the garage door up about four inches. Eulis forced open the door and they found mother on the floor, dead. They assumed she'd had a heart attack and called the funeral home to come pick up the body.

When the funeral home workers undressed mother to begin the embalming process, they found four bullet holes in her chest and called the sheriff, an elected official who was more politician than law officer, and who badly botched the entire investigation. Mother's body was sent to McAlester for an autopsy.

After we had told and retold the story dozens of times, someone finally took me to Daddy's house. Since Mother had finally filed for divorce six months earlier, Daddy was living in a tiny rented house in town, and had become engaged to Virginia, the woman he had been openly dating for the last year. I arrived to find Daddy and Virginia there alone.

Daddy immediately told me I would not be staying there with him since the house was so small. Instead, I would stay with his sister and brother-in-law, Virgie and Archie. I was at his house only a few minutes before he and Virginia drove me to Archie and Virgie's and dropped me off. My brothers still had not arrived.

The events of the evening had left me stunned. I barely knew my own name, much less what was going on around me. Virgie fed me, listened to me ask questions for which she had no answers, and tucked me into bed, where I collapsed from exhaustion.

The next morning, Daddy and my two brothers and their families arrived at Archie and Virgie's, and we began the torturous process of trying to figure out what was going on. Daddy claimed that he was with Virginia when Mother died, but admitted that the sheriff had confiscated both his .22 pistol and his .22 rifle. That was the first time I realized he was a suspect.

But as he held court in Virgie's living room, I was struck by his demeanor. This was a Daddy I had never seen before. He was running on pure adrenaline; his eyes unnaturally large and bright, his statements and stories even more exaggerated than usual. It was as if he were determined to act natural, but in so doing was only calling attention to himself. He was extremely nervous, but showed no sign at all of grief over the death of this woman he had lived with for twenty-six years. The longer he performed, the angrier I became.

My two brothers, Marvin and Jamey, were as stunned as I was, and all three of us had dozens of questions. But answers were not forthcoming. We later decided that the Oklahoma Bureau of Investigation officers who had taken over the investigation from the sheriff were giving us no information because we were with Daddy and his relatives. If we wanted to know what was going on, we had to go to Violet's and talk to mother's sisters.

Eventually, we learned that Mother had been shot with two longs and two shorts from the same gun. I thought that was strange, but apparently it was a common practice among shooters and hunters.

The first two bullets struck mother's heart, killing her instantly. The other two bullets struck her lungs. None of the bullets had exited her body, and the instant death meant there was no blood loss. Whoever had killed her was a good shot; even at close range, it's not easy to make four shots like that.

She had clearly been murdered.

Mother had attended Sunday evening church at the First Baptist Church, where she had been a member for more than twenty years, and where my brothers and I had all been baptized. Across the highway, Stanley Holt's wife, Lilian, saw mother's garage door go up and the light go on about 7:20 p.m., as Lilian was washing dishes. Investigators later speculated that the killer was waiting in the garage, and after she drove inside and stepped out of the car, shot her from no more than five feet away. Her body fell on the automatic garage door opener, which closed the door and turned off the light. But the killer was now trapped inside, and climbed up on the trunk of mother's car to grab the cord and disengage the automatic opener. Then, the killer stepped off the car, manually opened the door, and disappeared into the night.

There was a large, clear handprint and several foot scrape marks on the trunk lid, but for some reason they were never collected for evidence. A half-pint whiskey bottle was found on the ground by the trashcan, outside the garage's back door, but it was never collected as evidence or tested for fingerprints. The sheriff's deputies snickered that Mother must've been having a nip or two in secret, but everyone in the family knew that Mother had never had a drink of any kind in her life.

Mother's car door was open when her body was found, and Aunt Dorothy picked up her purse from the front seat and later gave it to me. No one ever asked whether she'd had a purse, or what had happened to it, and it never occurred to me to mention it to one of the investigators. In the end, it was the missing purse that convinced the investigators that the killer had been a bum walking the highway looking for a warm place to sleep. He had forced his way into the garage, they said, been startled when Mother arrived home, then had taken advantage of the chance to steal her purse and run. Her death had never been intended, they thought.

But it was months before we ever got that information. Meanwhile, Mother had been killed three days before Thanksgiving, so we held her funeral the day after Thanksgiving, at the First Baptist Church. The crowd was huge—standing room only, including news media representatives from as far away as Tulsa. Mother had taught school in Haskell County for more than thirty years, and was widely known and respected as one of the best elementary teachers around. Hundreds of her past students were in the church for her funeral.

I had decided to have a closed casket because I didn't want people gawking at my Mother, making her into some sideshow freak. Mother's sister, Ethel, objected loudly to that decision, but we held a private viewing for family at the funeral home, so I ignored her objections. We buried her at the Stigler cemetery in the plot next to her deceased parents.

For months after the funeral, Marvin and Jamey and I pretended that everything was normal when we saw Daddy, but we were all uncomfortable for a long time. As soon as the OSBI investigators decided that an itinerant bum had killed Mother, Daddy and Virginia married, less than four months after her death.

And Daddy treated Virginia the way we all wished he'd treated Mother but never did. He showered her with gifts of all kinds. He built a new home for her. He treated her as if she were a queen. In reality, she was his servant, just as Mother had been, but there was a difference. Where Mother had always resented the way Daddy treated her, for Virginia, Daddy was the king of the world and could do no wrong. Where Mother had fought Daddy on so many things, chiefly his financial decisions, Virginia gladly supported him in all his many ventures, and together they accumulated great financial success and became very wealthy.

But by the time I returned to Sand Springs and my teaching duties and directing activities, I had fallen apart emotionally. I had exercised my public persona during the funeral and its aftermath, but when I got home and was alone, I cried constantly, and worried about the future of my family. Mother was gone. Daddy had moved on. There were still serious questions about who was Mother's killer, and I made a conscious decision to go along with the transient bum theory, in part to maintain contact with my two brothers. To my way of thinking, they were now the only family I had left, and they came with Daddy. But way in the back of my mind, I still had questions about the possibility of Daddy's involvement, and although I continued to visit and participate in family events, it was always with that public persona intact.

So we all continued with our lives, and all gathered occasionally at Daddy and Virginia's for a holiday or family weekend. And as we got to know Virginia, it was impossible not to love her. She was a warm, loving woman who wholly supported Daddy in everything he did. Most of all, she loved him completely. He was happier than we had ever seen him, and we were all grateful for that. And she believed her mission in life was now to make him happy, whatever that took.

That didn't mean that we didn't regret Mother's death, but it was clearer than ever that Daddy and Mother never should have married in the first place. They had made each other miserable for more than twenty-six years.

But the residual effects of Mother's death stayed with me as I returned to work, and I functioned at less than half my previous effectiveness. *Carousel,* my current theater production, had been faltering before Mother died. I was over my head, my inexperience having caught up with me, and nothing I tried was working. Now, I was simply unable to continue the charade and cancelled the production rather than put on a less-than-outstanding show. RT agreed with my decision, but he was the only person who did; parents, students, and my principal howled in outrage and demanded explanations, but there were none. I simply couldn't finish what I had started.

My depression affected my students, and our contest success of the previous year completely disappeared. We brought home no trophies for the entire school year—unheard of at this school. With no play in production and lagging interest in contest work, there was nothing upon which to build lesson plans and I became desperate to fill the class hours. Eventually, all my classes descended into study halls and make-work and I was helpless to turn that situation around.

I didn't know until much, much later that I desperately needed grief counseling. For the moment, I just stumbled along the best I could. But the best at that time was a pitiful imitation of the previous year's successes.

Finally, I admitted to myself what a mess I'd made of the year, and turned in my letter of resignation. The principal told me, "That's good, Pat, because I wasn't going to renew your contract."

The mystery of Mother's murder was never solved. Over the years, both Marvin and I separately contacted the District Attorney for updates, but there were never any answers and the murder remained in the cold case files.

Marvin and I never talked about what we had learned, if anything. In fact, it was not until more than forty years later that I even knew about his contact with the officials.

At one point, many years later, Dorothy told Jamey and me that while the commotion was still going on at Mother's house, and she and Eulis were still there, Daddy had arrived in his truck and wanted to know "what's wrong with Willie?" There was a local drunk named Peanut something in the truck with Daddy. Several years later Peanut fell out of his boat at the lake, hit his head and drowned. A popular rumor at that time was that he had been Mother's killer. But that was just pure speculation.

In my own mind, I believed that Daddy was somehow responsible for Mother's death, but he had not been the one who pulled the trigger. I thought he was too much a coward to kill her himself, no matter how badly he wanted to be with Virginia. I thought it was possible that he had arranged for his brother, James, to do it for him, but in the end, I thought he might have hired Peanut to do it, and then killed Peanut to keep him quiet. I'll never know the real truth, however, since all the persons who knew the truth are deceased.

But my already rocky relationship with Daddy was never the same, and whatever semblance of neutrality we had maintained up to that point disappeared completely. And with Mother gone I had no anchor, and descended further and further into depression until I was barely able to function.

I remember few details from those months right after Mother's death; it's all very fuzzy in my mind. Very little about that time seems real; it's as if it were all a dream and I was just a minor player. Several professionals have told me that I was in shock, so it is not surprising that the details are so fuzzy.

Chapter 15

But now, in addition to being depressed, I was also unemployed, or soon would be. One day at church I explained to RT and my pastor what had happened, and the pastor wondered if I would consider working for a summer as a counselor at Ridgecrest, the summer religious retreat owned and run by the Southern Baptist Convention.

"They only pay minimum wage," he explained, "but it would give you a chance to spend a lot of time with God and renew your faith. What do you think?"

"That works for me," I said. Three weeks later, I had been accepted as an entry-level worker and was to report to the compound east of Asheville, North Carolina, the day after Memorial Day.

As a regular church-going Baptist, of course I had heard of Ridgecrest, as well as the similar compound in New Mexico. But that's all I knew about the place—it was a summer religious retreat, like an ongoing revival, with a different group of campers each week.

The reality was a huge surprise.

I knew something was different as soon as I arrived, after two days' travel, in my shorts and T-shirt. Everyone else was wearing jeans or dresses. *Oops!* Nonetheless, I checked in and picked up my employee packet, then found my assigned dorm room, where I dumped my suitcase on the bed and ripped open the employee packet to find out what I needed to know. *What?* I was to be a *dining room supervisor*, at the lofty pay of seven dollars an hour, much higher than the advertised minimum wage.

But I knew nothing about being a dining room supervisor! What in the world would I do? I had just jumped back into the fire and my heart sank. What was to be a renewal for me would be just another failure, the last thing in the world I needed right now.

Tears were running down my face as I sat there and stared at the papers, hoping beyond hope there was something else there I hadn't seen, when in walked an elderly woman with snow-white hair and the sweetest smile I had ever seen.

"How can I help you, sweetheart?" Her name was Ellen, she said, and she was the dorm counselor, assigned to help the workers adjust to our new lives.

"It says here I'm supposed to be a dining hall supervisor," I told her, "but I know absolutely nothing about that. I'm a school teacher!"

She laughed gently and patted my knee. "Oh, don't worry a bit, honey. There's a young woman here who has done that job for years, and she's going to train you. You'll love her—she's the sweetest thing. Her name is . . ." and she talked on and on about my trainer, until it finally sank into my addled brain what she was saying, and my tears finally dried. "Would you like to meet her? She's right down the hall. Come on, I'll introduce you."

With that, Ellen took my hand and led me down the hall to Stacy's room, where she introduced us, then left us alone to get acquainted. Thirty minutes or so later, I was convinced that everything would be fine and was looking forward to my new adventure.

Over the course of the summer I worked in the dining hall, supervising three hundred college students as they delivered family-style meals to two thousand guests three times a day. And I found my competent self again. I relearned, as I had to do over and over again, that I was a valuable, talented individual with loads of potential, if only I could overcome my poor self-esteem.

I attended every church service with the guests and other staff members, and immersed myself in the worship of God. When we were not in church or working, the women in our dorm spent time in the rocking chairs on the porch, singing hymns, telling each other the stories of our lives, and learning from each other. Everyone had a story, some more dramatic than others, but all had some version of overcoming great obstacles with the help of God's many miracles. I told my story in bits and pieces, and received love and respect from my fellow travelers. For that's exactly what we all were: travelers on the journey of life, each seeking and hopefully finding God's mercies.

Every two weeks or so, we would all load up in my car and make the twelve-mile trip to Asheville for supplies. One day, after the daily afternoon shower, we pulled into a mountaintop shopping center parking lot and as I turned east to park the car, we saw a full, double rainbow, with both ends touching the ground in two different valleys below us. We sat there nearly an hour, staring at that unbelievably beautiful, tranquil sight, amazed again at the beauties of God's world.

Another day, we took our afternoon off and drove up into the mountains above Ridgecrest after a rain, and experienced waterfall after waterfall cascading down over us as we passed by on the road below. And when we stopped at a roadside gift shop for local crafts, we realized we had ascended above the clouds and couldn't see the valley below. We felt we could reach out and touch the hand of God!

By the time I returned to Sand Springs at the end of summer, I knew with complete certainty that God would provide. I would find a job and would be able to support myself. And I would be able finally to put behind me years of self-doubt and destructive behavior, and fulfill my potential as a child of God.

Sure enough, the day I returned home, I called the personnel manager at National Tank Company and reminded him of his promise to put me to work. Not so coincidentally, he told me they had just been approved for a reorganization, and would need to fill a new position, that of secretary to the assistant vice president of employee relations. The job was definitely mine if I wanted it, and they would be more than delighted to have me back.

Chapter 16

I began my career in human resources in September of 1971, and never looked back. National Tank Company had been sold to Combustion Engineering, Inc., and was now C-E Natco. I was secretary to Wayne Snow, who had been hired from the accounting department to be the assistant vice president of employee relations.

On my first day of work, Wayne told me he didn't know anything about employee relations and would count on me to help him learn what it was all about.

"That's okay, Wayne," I said. "I don't know anything about being a secretary, either, so we'll just learn it all together." And that's exactly what we did.

My typing skills were still intact, and Wayne soon learned to lean on me for proofreading his correspondence and suggesting better ways to construct a sentence. I subscribed to professional journals and magazines, which I studied on my own time. He paid for my membership in the personnel management association and the training manager's association, and I attended all the meetings and took notes from every presentation. Each time I learned something new, I discussed it with Wayne, and together we figured out what we needed to do.

Wayne was an interesting man to work for. He'd never had a personal secretary before me, nor had I ever been a secretary, so we were both feeling our way along. But I did have a hard time with some of the "duties" he expected of his secretary.

For example, he thought secretaries should bring their bosses coffee whenever they asked. Unfortunately, he always seemed to ask when I was under deadline pressure.

One day in particular, Wayne, two other managers, and I had been working for days to finish and send a proposal to home office, and we were nearing the end. The deadline was that same day. I was frantically typing as fast as I could, the "final" draft, while Wayne and the other two managers kept revising what I had typed. In those days, there were no computers, but I did have an IBM Correcting Selectric typewriter. Even using the correction feature, however, page after page had to be typed over again after they made some change. The other two managers were constantly in and out of Wayne's office, which meant they went through my office dozens of times, talking constantly and disrupting my work.

In spite of the changes and interruptions, as we neared the end of the day, Wayne declared the draft finished, and the three men settled in his office to wait for me to finish the final revisions. I was working as hard and fast as I could, and Wayne was calling out to me about every five minutes, "How's it coming, Pat?"

Each time, I answered as nicely as I could, "Fine."

But when he called out, "Pat, would you bring us a cup of coffee, please?" I'd had it. I stopped typing, took a deep breath, and said, in as pleasant a tone as

I could manage, "Wayne, you can have your coffee, or you can have this proposal finished by five o'clock. Which would you prefer?"

Then, complete silence from Wayne's office. After a few moments, I returned to my typing. Another few minutes later, Wayne and the other two managers tiptoed through my office and out the door.

A few minutes before five o'clock, I put the finished and proofed proposal on Wayne's desk, just as he walked back in the door, alone. "Great! It's finished!" he said, and sat down to take one final look.

I waited until he approved and signed the document, and faxed it off to headquarters, before I gathered my things to leave for home.

Wayne stopped me on my way out the door.

"Pat, I want to apologize to you for the way I spoke to you today, and the way I've been treating you. It's not your responsibility to wait on me hand and foot, along with all your other duties, and I promise I'll never do that again, if you'll forgive me. Please?"

"Of course, Wayne. Thank you for seeing that. I'll see you tomorrow."

The next day around mid-morning, Wayne paused at the door on his way out.

"Pat, I'm going for coffee. Can I bring you something?"

"No thanks, Wayne, but thanks for asking."

And for the next five years that we worked together, Wayne never went after coffee without offering to bring me some, and I never went for a coke without offering to bring him one.

While I was at C-E Natco, I learned about the Civil Rights Act of 1964 and the recent requirements for Affirmative Action Plans almost simultaneously with a corporate request to see our AAP, which, of course, did not exist. Within three weeks, I had done the research and put one together, and Wayne sent it in with a plea for mercy. To our surprise, my plan was praised, and was even used as the model plan for the entire corporation. I felt an enormous sense of accomplishment.

That plan resulted in my first promotion, from secretary to administrative assistant, and I hired my replacement and trained her. Once she was in place, I was assigned more, higher-level HR work, and helped design the company's first fully realized compensation plan. That came back from corporate with more kudos and another huge pay increase. I was feeling more and more confident.

As time passed and I grew more confident, I became more and more frustrated with the spelling and grammar errors in the monthly newsletter that was published by the marketing department. One day I marked all the obvious errors in red and placed the copy on Wayne's desk without comment. Two days later, I was named the first full-time editor of the marketing newsletter, much to the chagrin of the marketing manager, who thought I was an upstart trying to take his job. Nothing could have been further from the truth; I just wanted not to be embarrassed by our in-house publications.

By the end of my first eighteen months at C-E Natco, I had been promoted again, and was now the first exempt-level female in the history of that company. My responsibilities included affirmative action and EEO compliance, monitoring and reporting on President Nixon's wage freeze, monitoring and reporting on compliance with the compensation plan, editing and publishing the twelve-page marketing newsletter each month, updating and posting thirty-six company bulletin boards twice a week. I was also administering the company's tuition reimbursement program and keeping all the policies and procedures updated as needed, a nearly full-time job by itself.

One day I foolishly suggested that the company provide some time management training for the management staff. The next day, Wayne told me my new job had been approved, and I was now the company training administrator, with a new pay level. The only hitch was that I had to carry with me all my current responsibilities. "Who should I train to do all the other things?" I asked.

"That's not part of the deal," he responded.

I was already working twelve and fourteen hours a day, and since I had been made exempt from overtime I was making less money than I had two years prior. And then, using the marketing newsletter as a reason, the marketing manager made a plea for me to be transferred from employee relations to the marketing department, and I now reported to the man who believed I was trying to replace him.

And things went from bad to worse. In addition to everything else, John expected me to do his secretarial work. I flatly refused; there simply weren't enough hours in the day. Of course, he was furious, but soon he hired a fulltime secretary, a young woman who was a Farah Fawcett wanna-be. For a short time, I was able to concentrate on meeting my own deadlines. Then John and his secretary embarked on what I believed was a passionate affair, and the situation deteriorated again.

John's secretary was only moderately competent. She could type, and she could take instructions. But her finished work was always marred by smears of makeup from her fingers, and was full of typos and other spelling errors. John began giving her "finished" work to me to re-do. I did the work, but deeply resented every moment of it, and let John know in no uncertain terms.

One day a co-worker told me that she had overheard John, in the downstairs club the evening before, loudly joking that I was "jealous of (his secretary) because she has big boobs and Pat doesn't."

That was the end. I simply would not tolerate that situation any longer. After months and months of trying to adjust either the work responsibilities or the pay, and being unsuccessful, the affair between John and his secretary was the straw that broke the camel's back. I eventually found another job outside the company. I had been with C-E Natco for five and a half years, and had accomplished amazing things in that time. But by the time I left, I felt only bitterness toward the company because of the way I felt they had taken advantage of me.

The day of my departure, company president Jud Lowd stopped by to tell me goodbye. He told me what a great job I had done and how much the company would miss me, and asked me one more time to stay. When I refused, he actually reached across the desk and *patted me on the head* as he turned to leave. "Take care, Pat. We'll miss you." Pat, pat, pat. I almost killed him before he got out the door. *That condescending, patronizing son of a …!*

But I really felt good about myself and the work I had done at C-E Natco. I had faced every new challenge head on, and had successfully completed every one, learning tons of new skills along the way. For the first time in my life, I could hold my head up and be myself twenty-four hours a day, every day, and seldom had a doubt about my competence, skills, or ability to be successful.

Chapter 17

I was never beautiful, but after the successes at C-E Natco I felt confident enough that both men and women seemed to want to be with me. I dated occasionally, when I met a single man, and spent some time with other single women, but no longer needed the approval of anyone to feel good about myself.

The problems between me and Daddy, however, still persisted for many years, to my great regret.

Because of his lack of business experience, Daddy never understood what I did to make a living. While I was teaching school, he always told people that I was a school teacher in Tulsa, and that was fine.

But when I went to work at C-E Natco, he would tell anyone who would listen that I was "working as a secretary at some company in Tulsa. They sure pay her good for a secretary," he would say. "I don't know what she has to do to make that much money, but whatever it is, she's sure paid good." I was always embarrassed by that description, and told him so many times, but his story never changed. As I moved up into management positions and made more and more money, in his eyes, I always remained a secretary, doing whatever was necessary to earn my pay. To his mind, that was a great compliment.

And I never stopped trying to please him, to be Daddy's girl.

One time, when I had begun to accumulate some savings, Daddy called to tell me he needed my help. He wanted to buy some land between Stigler and Keota, he said, out by the lake, where he wanted to build a new home for Virginia. But the woman who owned the property, he said, wouldn't sell it to him. She didn't like him.

So, he wanted me to buy the property for him. It was ten acres right on the lake, and included a house. I could rent the house for some income, he said, and he would take care of that for me. But after the sale was final, I would sell the western-most five acres to him, and he would build Virginia's house there. I had reservations, but agreed to go take a look.

It seemed like a no-lose proposition. The property was on Highway 9, at Keota Landing, right at the edge of the lake formed by part of the Kerr-McClellan Navigation System of locks and dams. That part of the lake was a popular fishing and boating site, and there was a place nearby where coal was loaded onto river barges making their way down to New Orleans or up to Tulsa.

The property was elevated from the highway, and had a great view to the west and south. The part to the north was wooded, and when cleared could make several more home sites. The asking price was within what I could afford. I agreed with Daddy's proposal, and bought the property, using money from some of my CDs.

Before the ink was dry on the bill of sale, Daddy had already started the foundation on Virginia's new house, and he never looked back. He called me a few days later and told me he had rented the house that was already on the property, and he would send the rent check in a few days. I never received the rent check, or any other rent checks. Three months into the deal, the rent house burned to the ground. Daddy said he thought the renters had skipped because they couldn't pay the rent.

He later admitted he had received a check from the insurance company, but he had used it on construction of the new house. I never saw a nickel of it.

Before long, Daddy had finished Virginia's house and they moved in. He built and sold another new house, just to the east of the one that had burned. He rebuilt the burned house and sold it. He built and sold another new house on the hillside just above the others. And all that time he was telling me he would pay me for my investment in the property "as soon as I get a little cash flow."

That never happened, and I was never paid, or reimbursed, for my purchase of the original ten acres. But Daddy had launched his building career, and for the next twenty or so years built and sold dozens of homes in Haskell County, and made a ton of money doing it.

Eventually, I gave up on ever recouping my investment, and chalked it up to my own stupidity in trusting Daddy. I had willingly let him take advantage of me, because I so badly wanted him to love me. Unfortunately, I never believed that to be true.

Many, many years later, after Daddy's health was failing and he had been in a nursing home for some time, he told me one day that, "I done something to you that time I never shoulda done." That's the closest he ever came to an apology. Unfortunately, I never understood which incident he was referring to.

During the final three years of his life, Daddy's escalating verbal abuse of me and my two brothers became so bad that I finally refused to see him at all. Marvin, bless his God-loving heart, never abandoned him, but I hadn't seen Daddy in at least two years when he finally died of kidney disease and heart failure.

But I had learned to forgive him years earlier, in order to move on with my life. And after that awful public seminar fiasco, I finally faced the truth about the way I had been living all those years, forgave myself for all my bad behavior, let go the grief and guilt over my deal with the devil, and with a lot of hard work, moved on with my life.

Chapter 18

I rose steadily in the ranks, until, fewer than ten years after exchanging teaching for human resources, I became senior vice president and director of human resources for a three billion dollar bank with 1,800 employees and twenty-two direct reports, and reported directly to the Chief Executive Officer.

My human resources career lasted for more than forth-three years.

Of course, there were occasional set-backs and stumbles along the way—no one is perfect, after all. But I became a well-known and well-respected professional in my chosen career, sought out as a mentor, and asked to lead other professionals in our certification endeavors and conferences.

I had gained valuable experience in the legal aspects of human resources and was frequently consulted by senior management who wanted my guidance about some sticky situation or other.

I had managed, or personally performed, almost every job function in HR, including recruiting and hiring; employee relations; training and development; compensation and benefits; compliance, and payroll. And if I didn't know what to do, I knew where to find the answers.

Along the way, I earned a Master of Science degree in adult education, and taught graduate level

HR and Management courses for Webster University for more than fifteen years.

And I began writing books, trying to teach others the things I had learned the hard way, through the school of hard knocks. My first book, *Hiring Right: A Business Blueprint for Lower Turnover and Higher Profits*, was a compilation of what I had learned during the course of my research for the Masters, when I validated the employment process for the company where I worked at the time. I worked on that book for nearly ten years before finally publishing it in 2004; the first printing sold out in less than two months. I updated and published the Second Edition in late 2014, and as fast as the career field is changing, I believe there may be several more editions coming down the road.

I also wrote hundreds of newsletters, video training scripts, training programs, and newspaper columns.

Eventually I began also writing fiction, and to date have published three novels and several novellas, or short novels, along with short stories. In all of my fiction work, I use situations I have personally experienced during my career, and weave them into stories with completely fictional characters, places, and people. Using my career as fodder for the writing means I'll never lack for subjects—it's only a question of which ones to write first.

Chapter 19

I'm reminded again of that day in the garden, after my humiliating speech, when I broke down in the yard.

I turned away from the ugly, rotting stump, leaned my head against the handle of the hoe, and cried. Salty tears washed down my cheeks, leaving streaks in the accumulated dirt. I used my dirty shirt tail to wipe my face, but the tears kept coming. I cried long and hard, for all the mistakes I had made over the years and for all the wonderful successes I had never let myself celebrate. I cried for the many lonely years when I had endured self-doubt and feelings of worthlessness. I cried for the child, the teenager and the young woman who had never learned she didn't need Daddy's approval to be a worthy person in her own right. And I finally understood the truth of my own teachings. *I no longer needed to blame Daddy for my own failures. I could fail or succeed without his approval, and as scary as that thought was, it was also wonderfully liberating.*

Eventually the tears subsided, leaving me gasping for breath but feeling cleansed and whole for the first time in my life. I sat in the shade of the deck for more than an hour, my mind blank and peaceful at last.

I was startled from my own reverie by the raucous, insistent sound of two bluejays overhead. I located the birds in one of the trees and finally saw the cause of all the commotion. Three young had fledged and were making their way across the yard, loudly protesting each step of the way. Comically disheveled in their new feathers, the disreputable-looking fledglings fluttered and stuttered from twig to branch, to limb, to tree, one adult in front and the other bringing up the rear. The spectacle continued for several minutes, until the parading squad disappeared into the trees in an adjacent yard, their progress marked by the diminishing cacophony.

I began to laugh out of sheer delight. *Life does go on. Even that rotting old stump supports new life for the creatures that feed off its decomposing matter.* And finally I understood the mystery of my failed seminar performance.

For my entire life, I had lived with a constant fear of failure. Daddy's messages had taken hold in my heart, but to the world at large, I presented the image of a talented, self-confident woman who lived her messages of hope. I had been living a lie, and when I made that fateful seminar presentation I discovered I just could not do it any longer.

Now, I resolved, for the very last time, that my life would only be a reflection of my true self. *No more lies. No more pretending to be someone I was not.*

The stress left my shoulders and face and I cried again, this time in relief rather than grief. Relief that I could finally, after all these years, be comfortable enough with myself that it would no longer be necessary to present a false persona to the world.

I could be myself! I no longer needed to be Daddy's girl and suffer his abuse; no longer needed to hide myself behind a façade of achievement and busyness.

Elated, I surveyed the yard one last time with satisfaction, then turned and went into the house to make something wonderful to eat and to begin my new life.

Chapter 20

I finally retired in 2008, and now happily spend my time in retirement writing about my human resources management experiences, and also writing novels. My nonfiction writing is devoted to helping others to succeed in their careers and to avoid some of the mistakes I made. My fiction stories and novels are simply for fun, but they all deal in some way with things that are important to me, like the difficulties experienced by veterans and others with PTSD and traumatic brain injuries, or the horrible international sex trafficking rings, or sexual abuse, or sex discrimination against women. I try to get my points across in entertaining ways, but still get the point across.

I hope and pray that readers of this memoir will learn from my journey of self-discovery. I hope you will see that, while I've lived through many difficult times and traumatic events, I've come through whole and happy, and you can do that as well.

I want to share with you some of the things I've learned. I hope you'll find a nugget or two that will help you along your journey.

First, Learn to Love Yourself

Please do not allow yourself to believe that you are not good enough, or pretty enough, or thin enough …. You are more than enough, just as you are. God created you in His image, and that means you're perfect just being yourself.

That doesn't mean you can't learn new skills, or make yourself the best *you* that you can be.

But do not allow your self-image to be determined by anyone else but you. Do not try to mold yourself to meet someone else's notion of who or what you should be. You're more than enough, just as you are.

Graciously Accept Help

There's no shame in admitting it when you encounter a new situation you've never faced before. Take Johnnie Wray's lessons to heart, believe in yourself and your God, and do your very best to live up to His expectations. When you come across a Johnnie Wray, celebrate her and her life, and accept what she teaches you with love and appreciation.

Johnnie's best lesson for me was that I had the potential to be whomever and whatever I wanted to be, if I only believed in myself enough. That's true for you, too.

Seek Professional Help

Professional-level counseling helped me learn to forgive my mother for not protecting me from Daddy, to forgive Daddy for his abusive treatment of me as a child and adult, and to forgive myself for the misplaced feelings of guilt and self-recrimination concerning my own mistakes. Without that professional help at key times along the way, I would never have been able to forgive those who had wronged me, or to forgive myself for my own bad behavior.

Never Stop Learning

I don't remember where I heard it, but I eventually learned the hard way that if you're not learning, you're dying. *There is no such thing as too expert in your field.*

Learning—about oneself, about living with others in this world, and about the world at large, gives us a broader, more comprehensive perspective than just our own lives. Only through this broader perspective can we ever really begin to understand ourselves.

One very good way to learn is through membership in professional associations. Their educational programs, and certification programs, will teach you new information and skills you can apply in many ways.

For example, through my membership in the personnel management and training associations, I eventually served as president of those groups, and worked as program chair for two regional conferences. All of those experiences taught me management and leadership skills I still use every day.

Find Your True Passion

It took me a long time to learn this lesson, but I finally did learn the hard way that only by following my true passion in life would I ever be happy and content. For me, that meant teaching other adults. I was never happier, or more productive, or more effective, than when I was writing or teaching a management development program, writing or producing a video training program, or writing a book to teach others what I had learned about hiring employees.

Only then could I leave my dual persona behind, and become myself twenty-four hours a day. Only then did the migraine headaches and stomach ulcers go away. And only then could I stop worrying about being found a fraud, relax, and enjoy my work.

Finally, **Serve Others**

Many, many management experts over the years have taught that only by helping others achieve their goals, will you ever achieve your own goals. I believe that is true.

No matter your job or your position in life, seek out ways to be of service to others. In that way, you will be fulfilled and at peace with yourself. I hope and pray that will be true for you.

My husband believes that his mission in life is to give life to others, as Jesus teaches. With that always in his mind, he may have moments of distress, but he never questions the reason for his existence. I'm trying to learn that lesson from him.

As I said earlier in this manuscript, it has taken me many years to finish writing this book. In many ways it was painful; many of the memories were extremely difficult to experience again. In other ways, however, it was uplifting to my spirit. After all, I did persevere, and have at last learned to love and accept myself just as I am. What more could I possibly ask?

May God bless you, and hold you in his loving embrace.

Acknowledgments

I would never have been able to finish writing this story without the help and support of my family and friends, especially the members of the Green Country Ruff Riters, a writers' support group in Poteau, and my husband, Jerry. I have struggled to get it done for more than ten years now, and finally, it is! I also want to acknowledge the very special, specific help of editor and writing coach extraordinaire, Shayla Eaton, of Curiouser Editing. Shayla is a fellow Okie who truly understands the language and colloquialisms of Oklahoma, and didn't force me to do a complete rewrite to remove all those local references.

Many, many thanks to all of you, and much love to Jerry, for your amazing love and support.

About the Author

Pat Kelley, MS, SPHR, recently retired after a 43-year career in human resource management. While she was still working, Pat earned her Master of Science degree in adult education, and taught at the graduate level more than fifteen years. After she retired from human resources, Pat began writing books and articles, telling the stories that had haunted her for years. Her fiction books are often suggested by actual situations that she and her colleagues experienced. Her nonfiction books are based on her own personal research and work experiences.

She is the 2008 recipient of the Arkansas Society for Human Resource Management's Lifetime Achievement Award. She is the author of dozens of articles, case studies, and newsletters, as well as the nonfiction how-to book *Hiring Right: A Business Blueprint for Lower Turnover and Higher Profits, Second Edition,* published in December, 2014.

Pat is also an accomplished speaker and teacher, and with her engaging style, real-life stories, and examples, she has presented many hundreds of keynotes, management development programs, seminars, and workshops over the years. She is lifetime certified as a Senior Professional in Human Resources (SPHR).

In addition to her writing activities, Pat loves taking photos of her flowers and the birds that visit her feeders each year. With her husband, she enjoys travel, and often writes about her adventures, such as when she hiked across the caldera of Hawaii's Kilauea volcano.

Addendum

Daddy's Girl is a memoir. As such, the incidents and people depicted here are truthful and factual, as least as far as I can recall. I felt and recall many of the things that happened much differently than my brothers, because of our different experiences. But as my older brother said, "they're my memories." So, if you wonder at the accuracy of reported events and conversations, for example, please remember that these incidents are indelibly burned into my memory. I did check and verify facts whenever possible, but many of the people mentioned in this book are no longer living, so it was not possible to verify every single one.

Some names of individuals have been changed, to or not mentioned at all, to protect their privacy. Other actual names have been used, to acknowledge the major contributions people have made in my life. I beg forgiveness if I have offended anyone by use, or no use, of their name.

If there are errors of fact, please blame only me. I tried very hard to get everything correct, but to the extent I did not, please bring those errors to my attention so that I can make corrections as soon as possible. Thank you.

Email me at pat@patkelleyauthor.com.

Connect with the Author:

http://www.patkelleyauthor.com

https://www.facebook.com/Pat-Kelley-Author-206554642886952/

email: pat@patkelleyauthor.com

Nonfiction Books:

Lessons Learned: Cases from 43 Years in HR

Hiring Right: A Business Blueprint for Lower Turnover and Higher Profits, Second Edition

Coming soon: *Leadership Basics for New Supervisors*

Fiction Books:

Journey to Love

Rich Mountain

Payback

Homecoming

Coming Soon:

Short Stories *Stranger in Dawes Creek* and *Kidnapped!* Coming June, 2016

Witteville, short story, in *Green Country Stories* published by GCRR, summer, 2016, edited by Pat Kelley

Artists and Authors of Green Country, coming fall, 2016

All of Pat's books are available through her Amazon author's page.

Go to www.amazon.com/patkelleyauthor.

www.ingramcontent.com/pod-product-compliance
Lightning Source LLC
LaVergne TN
LVHW051500070426
835507LV00022B/2856